Love My Children

LOVE MY CHILDREN

AN AUTOBIOGRAPHY

by

Rose Butler Browne, Ph.D.

and

James W. English

Meredith Press

NEW YORK

Second printing, September, 1969

SBN : 696-69380-1
Library of Congress Catalog Card Number : 69-19048
Manufactured in the United States of America for Meredith Press

CONTENTS

PART I

NEW ENGLAND

Chapter 1

HARVARD

All my life I have been armed to the teeth with security and self-assurance. These twin gifts, my inheritance from a loving family, have given me a value system which has seemed to be equal to every challenge in my life, with perhaps one exception. That would be the time I took the oral examination for my doctorate at the Graduate School of Education, Harvard University.

I had encountered no prejudice at Harvard. However, that should not have blinded me to the fact that the first and only Negro to earn a similar degree in education at Harvard was Dr. Howard Long of Washington, D. C., back in 1928. Also, although women took courses in the Graduate School of Education, I was the only woman in the department's doctorate program in 1937. Up till then less than a dozen women had succeeded in this doctorate program.

Of course, not only was I a woman, but, to complicate matters, a Negro.

Nothing had occurred to make me at all apprehensive, and when the day of my examination arrived, I was much too excited to look for storm signals.

The calendar showed early spring. The sky and the land had been washed clean of the gray blanket of winter, and although not yet warm, the air held pleasing promise. I was so enthusiastic, I wanted to dash across the Harvard Yard to my appointment; but I refrained from doing anything so undignified.

Naturally, I expected to get battered around a bit by the doctorate committee. This happened to everyone. Fellow students and the typists in the Graduate School were all pulling for me. For weeks they had offered words of encouragement and last-minute bits of advice. Undoubtedly the most helpful tip of all was, "Girl, don't wear a tight girdle."

But I wasn't afraid. I had a record of good grades at Cambridge. I had been elected to the Honor Society. My research project had been carefully programmed under the direction of my faculty adviser, the eminent educational psychologist Dr. Walter Fennell Dearborn. At my oral examination Dr. Dearborn would appear with me. Beyond this backing stood my family support, for we Butlers stuck together.

The doctorate committee of five would be moderated by the Dean of the Graduate School, Dr. Henry Wyman Holmes. I had studied philosophy under his tutorage; in fact, I knew personally all the members of this committee I would face in the Dean's Conference Room in Lawrence Hall.

Arriving early at the hall, I took a seat on one of the plain benches on the first floor and awaited my summons. Not a

4

single vestige of doubt troubled my mind as to whether I had covered all the bases. I had.

Sunlight streamed through the leaded glass windows and warmed the rich woods of the wainscoted wall behind me. The portraits of the James brothers, Henry and William, whose minds had been honed to intellectual excellence at the university, looked down on me from illuminated niches in this wall. The historic significance and the academic atmosphere of Harvard University was much in evidence.

I had first come to Harvard for summer school in 1930, soon after I had been appointed head of the Department of Education at Virginia State College, Petersburg, Virginia. This land-grant college had just taken over an in-service training program for teachers in the segregated Negro schools of Old Dominion. I was to supervise this work and came to Cambridge to take two courses in Public School Administration.

That summer happened to be the three hundredth anniversary of the founding and continuous occupancy of the city of Boston. For this occasion the city's great institutions of education and culture offered many special programs, most of which required some knowledge of the arts if they were to be fully appreciated. For instance, each morning before class I sat in Appleton Chapel and fed my soul with the music of the great classical composers, presented in a series of magnificent organ recitals. I made the rounds of concerts, most of them free, at the main library, the various museums and art galleries, all places of loving childhood memory, for Boston was my place of birth.

Needless to say I loved that summer and sought eagerly

5

an opportunity to return. I was back again during the academic school year of 1933-1934, and again the following year.

This was the period immediately after the United States Supreme Court had handed down its historic Gaines Decision (1934), and momentous changes were occurring among the South's Negro colleges. The Gaines Decision did not invalidate the Federal Government's educational guidelines of that day—separate but equal education for Negroes, but the court's ruling made it all but impossible to maintain such racial separation. The key point in the Gaines Decision required the Southern states to provide equal education for Negroes *at all levels,* up to and including the doctorate program. The price of racial segregation had escalated.

The traditional role-playing guise of the patronizing Southern politician and education administrator had become untenable. The end of the old order of things was opening new doors to the Negro, doors which we had not known existed before.

For instance, I learned that states have something called "contingent funds." Most state-sponsored white educational institutions in the South were willing to do almost anything, even forgo new funds, rather than risk having Negroes seek enrollment on their campuses. Therefore, many states, including Virginia, dipped heavily into these contingent funds to set up crash programs to upgrade the faculty of their Negro schools. Improving the level of the faculty became the initial step in preparing these schools to meet the minimum standards of accrediting bodies, whose approval was needed before higher degrees than Bachelor of Arts or Sciences could be conferred.

In Virginia (as elsewhere in the South) a massive scholarship program was started to send qualified Negro candidates "up North" to earn higher education degrees so that the faculty of Negro colleges could be upgraded for this new honors program. Unfortunately, it was nearly impossible to find qualified candidates.

I had already earned my Master's Degree at Rhode Island State University, but had a state grant handed me for the academic year 1933-1934, and again for the second semester of the following year, 1935-1936.

The President of Virginia State College had recognized in me a horse trained to work, and he did not look with favor upon my continued leave of absence from my teaching position at the college. This capable Negro administrator had used the panic of the state's white educational establishment following the Gaines Decision to secure for our campus a new science building, a lovely new library, new classroom buildings, and several greatly needed new dormitories. He had urgent need right then for qualified teachers, or even teachers who thought they were qualified. No one on his staff matched even those qualifications I already possessed.

This man knew also that Negroes who received an education beyond the average level of attainment usually stopped work to parade their intelligence before their admirers.

The scholarship program of the state of Virginia was basically a Master's program. Since I already had earned my Master's degree, my president wanted me teaching in the classroom right then. He did not want to wait for me to earn my doctorate degree.

While at Harvard University in 1933, I had taken a qualifying examination for the doctorate program. This two-day examination established one's qualifications to do advanced graduate work and to handle research problems. I had been

7

the only one of three women taking the examination to pass, while three of seven men had passed.

My president was able to delay my state funds for the first semester of the 1935-1936 academic year. I returned to Harvard for the second semester, despite his assurance that I would have a good job at Virginia State College as long as he remained president.

My pastor husband said, "You're this close, Rose. Go get your doctorate. What happens when that man isn't president any longer? He can't keep you from going to Harvard, just from coming back to Virginia State."

So in 1936-1937 I went back to Harvard University, but this time on a scholarship from the General Board of Education of the Rockefeller Foundation.

During all this time I knew there was nothing for me to be ashamed of in my work at Harvard. I loved Harvard, not only for the real challenge of its scholarship, but also for the bonus of its remarkable fellowship, such as afternoon teas. At 4:00 P.M., everything at Harvard's Graduate School of Education came to a halt and we had tea. Two students would pour the tea, which a maid had prepared. White royal biscuits were served, as they were the closest American approach to English crumpets.

Although about 150 of us were enrolled in the Graduate School of Education, probably more than a dozen countries were represented in this fellowship. It surprised me to discover how many of these foreign students had been misinformed about the American Negro by their native newspapers. Frequently I found myself assuring a foreign national that although the Negro American was discriminated against in this land of the free, generally his present condition represented an improvement over the former days of slavery.

For these students from other cultures, my assurances often contradicted their personal beliefs and previous information, and proved most difficult for them to comprehend fully. Their continued skepticism sometimes resulted in ridiculous misunderstandings.

I remember two Chinese students who went to a downtown Boston cafeteria and took seats, expecting to be waited on for their dinner order. Of course, they must have been oblivious to the line of people who were picking up trays and utensils and going through the serving line. However, these two Chinese students returned to their campus quarters unfed and bitterly convinced that America's policy of segregation against the world's colored races had been applied to them for the express purpose of embarrassing them if not actually starving them.

We all took turns explaining, and then laughing at them, before these two Chinese students professed to understand that there had been no racial overtones to their misadventure. I prayed that they did understand, for it is not easy when you are being laughed at.

I reacted to such situations as an American, which I have always considered myself to be, and such false criticism of my country hurt me personally.

Sometimes Americans, too, showed a lack of understanding. In a philosophy class taught by Dean Holmes, he asked us to prepare a course for a curriculum not then being taught.

"I suppose Mrs. Browne will prepare a course on Negro history," the Dean said.

"No sir, Dr. Holmes," I replied. "I would oppose a separate course on Negro history. The record of the many good things the Negro American has done for his country should be found in their proper sequence of events and recorded in all American history books. . . ."

"Perhaps the Negro arts, then," Dr. Holmes hastened to say. "Personally, I love to hear your people sing their Negro spirituals. I believe 'Swing Low' is my especial favorite."

"When you hear us sing 'Swing Low,' you've paid your money to hear a choir that aims to give you your money's worth," I said. "However, when that same choir sings 'Swing Low' to a Negro audience, they are telling the Lord how you white folks have been mistreating us. There's a difference!"

Another time, in my Systematic Study of School Systems course, we had a city planner as guest lecturer. I shall never forget. The poor man's name was Noland.

He put a diagrammatic map on the wall, and using a long pointer to call attention to his illustrations, started his lecture.

"Now here are the railroad tracks. On this side of the tracks you will note we have placed the business section, and behind that the better residential sections. Note the dispersal of schools, libraries, and other needed services. Now on the other side of the tracks we have the blighted areas, the Negroes, the refuse dumps, the cemeteries, etc. This way, because of careful city planning, one will never have a clash of cultures. . . ."

"My blessed redeemer!" I blurted out. "So that's how you do it!"

I think the poor man had not noticed that Harvard had admitted a Negro student to this class. He remained too flustered to reply to me. For several weeks, however, students

and faculty members greeted me by saying, "My blessed redeemer saith . . ."

I mention these things merely to show that I was known
on that campus, for I have never been afraid to speak out.
Also, in this predominantly white college society, my physical features caused me to stand out like a neon sign in the
desert.

This was my background at the time of my summons into
the Dean's conference room to face the oral-examination
committee probing my state of preparation for the doctorate
degree at Harvard University. Dr. Dearborn greeted me at
the conference-room door and ushered me to a chair before
a large table around which the committee sat. On the table
stood a brown wicker basket filled with bright red apples,
and he indicated I might help myself.

I shook my head. If I had opened my mouth wide enough
to bite into one of those apples, I'd never have been able to
talk to these men.

Dr. Dearborn laughed. "Mrs. Browne believes an apple
a day might keep the doctorate away."

This effort at humor fell flat. No one laughed.

For a period of two years I had been meeting with Dr.
Dearborn. The program of my research project had been
submitted to this committee only after this faculty adviser
had carefully checked and altered certain parts of my plan.
He had even had me check out the statistical methods with
Dr. Truman Kelly, the noted statistician. At no point in our
frequent student-adviser personal contacts and discussions
had I noted or been advised of the slightest reservation in regard to my research project or my own fitness for the
doctorate program. Dr. Dearborn had even asked, as a per-

sonal favor, that I tutor special reading disability cases at both the Arlington and the Cambridge Schools. At no time had there been the slightest friction in our academic relationship.

In fact, other than the cited incidents, the only other slightly racial overtone at Harvard involved a woman from one of my classes. We had at best a nodding sort of acquaintance. However, I happened to be standing beside her in the Dean's office when grades were posted. One of the woman's marks automatically necessitated her dismissal from the university.

These were the depression years, when jobs were scarce and many of my people were not only out of work but indeed hungry and destitute.

Bravely this woman fought back the bitter tears of her disappointment. Then she turned on me. She felt the need of a face-saving gesture, she being a white American and me a Negro American, but one who had passed this particular course.

"At least I have a job to return to!" the woman said defensively. "If someone had to be cut, better me than you."

Unwittingly she revealed among other things her ignorance, which is really the basis of all prejudice. To maintain a peer self-image in the face of such harsh disappointment, she had had to find a way to place herself above me, a Negro. It simply never occurred to her that I too might be on leave of absence from a high-paying college teaching job. She had never inquired, and I did not correct her. It would not have been the kind thing to do.

Other than such unwitting incidents, which every Negro knows and learns to expect, nothing had occurred during my stay at Harvard to indicate the slightest attitude of discrimination toward me.

The object of the oral examination is to present your proposed plan of research, to tell what you are trying to do, how you propose going about it, what other researchers have done in this field, what you expect to add to the knowledge of this subject area, to validate previous research done, and to tell what your results would do for the field of education.

My research project was in the field of remedial reading.

During my several years of teaching at Virginia State College, I had dealt with young people seeking an escape from the rural Negro ghettos of the South and from the emerging urban Negro ghettos of the North. The environment of both locales held a great deal of similarity—broken families, segregated education, poor housing, poor health, and in the young a growing frustration over their failure to find jobs and to earn any sort of livelihood.

One common measurement was the almost universal failure of Negro youths to reach their age norm in reading proficiency as measured on the national rating scales. This reading failure loomed large in my mind as a basic cause for poor grades and the inability of my children to change the course of their lives.

The accepted educational theory of that day held that remedial reading could only be taught on an individual basis, one to one—teacher to child. My practical experience told me that the numbers of Negro children in need of reading help ruled out such a limited method.

Also, during my student days at Rhode Island State Normal School, I had gained considerable exposure to the original Montessori method of preschool teaching. A member of the Rhode Island staff had been sent to Italy for a year to observe Madame Montessori's methods, which were originally planned for and executed in areas of extreme poverty. (This is quite unlike the middle-class, suburban society where today we find most Montessori and nursery schools.)

On her return from Italy, this teacher, Miss Clara Craig, was most enthusiastic about Madame Montessori's methods and results. Miss Craig adapted many of the ingenious teaching devices of the Montessori program to specific needs of our American culture, and especially favored those devices using kinesthetic surfaces.

In my opinion this Craig Method, as I called this Montessori adaptation, offered great promise to the culturally deprived Negro American child. These ingenious Montessori tools, plus other proposed learning stimuli—as opposed to purely environmental and social stimuli (also needed, however), I saw as a means of introducing the child of poverty to objects and devices beyond his present ken. Such an upgrading of background and culture, I reasoned, along with generous love from the teacher, would arouse a child's curiosity and be the forerunner to improved reading proficiency.

Ample reasons existed for believing the plan suitable for small-class situations. To prove this theory was the heart of my research project at Harvard University.

Working under the guidance of Dr. Dearborn, I proposed to study three basic groups.

The first, a normal classroom grouping, I called the "See and Say Method." This simply recognized that day's sight method for word recognition, a prereading preparation of the pupil.

For instance, the approved Massachusetts State reading readiness text of that day dealt with Baby Ray. Baby Ray, of course, was always shown as a white child. Baby Ray lived in a neat, new house; he had a pet dog and cat, numerous shiny new toys, and his father dressed in neat business suits and left each morning to go to work.

This was not the way of life in the slums, be the ghetto black or white or yellow or red.

The story line ran like this. "Baby Ray has a dog. Baby Ray has a cat. Baby Ray has two kittens."

The teacher would drill the class in the sight recognition of the name Baby Ray, and of such major new words as dog, cat, kitten. This started an eye vocabulary. From the child's home environment he had supposedly acquired an ear vocabulary. It was believed that this ear vocabulary would have conditioned the child to recognize proper use of predicates and small modifying words. However, this theory failed to take into consideration the home environment of the ghetto child, to whom "Baby Ray done got a dog" sounded just as proper as "Baby Ray has a dog."

No wonder my poor Negro children could not read! Even as they reached for their first book, a lack of middle-class background stifled the learning opportunity of the ghetto child. And how could a colored child identify with that rich, blond child, Baby Ray?

My second group, also a normal class grouping, would be taught by the Craig Method, the Americanized Montessori method with adaptations for special learning needs of the ghetto child.

The third group, which I called the Balance Group, was not a normal class grouping. This group would have the same chronological age and reading level—in other words, statistically the children would be on the same mean level. One half of this Balance Group would be taught by the See and Say Method and the other half by the Craig Method.

With the first two groups, both normal class groupings, it could be predicted that some wide variations would occur in individual pupil reading efficiencies. In both these groups we would compare initial and final status, to determine what measurable gains in reading efficiencies had been scored. The Balance Group's measurable gains would offer a statistical check against any wild and untypical marks in the other two groups, since such marks could be misleading in a statistical study. However, I needed these first two groups to represent the everyday classroom variations a teacher in the ghetto schools should expect.

I hoped to prove that the Craig Method, building a background of useful new concepts with children before they are taught to read, would dramatically increase reading proficiency. The concept is quite similar to present-day methods, made popular through Project Head Start teaching programs aimed at reading readiness.

The committee quickly passed over the "what" and "why" aspects of my project. However, when we discussed the "how"—how I planned to conduct the research, the committee's questions started in earnest.

"How can you be sure these test conditions will prevail? How can you keep your Balance Group uncontaminated? How can you be certain of your statistical findings?"

The trend of questioning came back to this single concern, which Dr. Dearborn and I had carefully worked out along guidelines insisted upon by him. I was left to explain and defend these choices, which was all right. I had not expected Dr. Dearborn to carry my burden.

However, when the committee finally said that I would have to conduct my research work in a test situation where I had complete and isolated control over the total school curriculum—in other words, where I could ensure that at no point in the children's other school courses would a test group be exposed to another reading concept, I expected Dr. Dearborn to say something. We had discussed this point many times, and had ruled it out as being desirable but impractical and quite unattainable. Therefore I now waited for Dr. Dearborn to say something.

"I didn't think she had too much," Dr. Dearborn said to the committee, never once looking at me.

I was floored! My grades were tops. If I didn't have too much, why hadn't he redirected me into more productive channels? If I didn't have too much, why had he wasted the time of this committee?

In situations like this, a Negro American has a second instinct, an acquired defense mechanism, which probes beneath the surface for the real reason why. Suddenly I commenced to see the light. I even felt a twinge of pity for Dr. Dearborn.

The establishment, that iconoclastic royal society of the Harvard Graduate School (to which Dr. Dearborn belonged) had made its decision. Their power play had trapped him. He had had to go along.

I never did discover whether my being a woman or a Negro had triggered their action. Most likely it was the combination.

Also, I could understand but not condone the establishment's concern. Since the Gaines Decision, Negroes had been pouring into Northern universities to seek advanced degrees. Despite the great depression, money was now available to qualified Negro teachers as never before. They flocked to Teacher's College, Columbia University, for instance, like bananas in bunches.

Most graduate schools don't really look at their students until they start on the doctorate program. The establishment's line of reasoning should have been made known to me in 1933, when I took my qualifying examination. Now, four years later, this committee faced an unpleasant task, although I am sure they considered it necessary for the good of Harvard. The leverage they used to invalidate my work was really quite simple: impose impossible conditions on the research project. Then it might reasonably be assumed that Mrs. Browne, finding the stipulated conditions impossible to attain, would quietly and peacefully go away. (I almost said, "and never darken their lives again.")

They didn't know Rose Butler Browne!

I was wounded! Dr. Dearborn's remark proved especially disappointing, for I had admired him. Although he was acting under unusual pressure, so was I.

While I struggled to clear my thoughts, these confident, self-assured, and polite white gentlemen, men of poise and culture, kept smiling and small-talking me.

"Have you any questions, Mrs. Browne?"

"What do you say, Mrs. Browne?"

At that particular moment my own security and self-assurance had vanished. I sat there like a helpless lump of clay, bewildered and crushed. I felt like bawling, and I am not a woman easily given to tears. My dreams of seven years were being wiped out through no fault of mine. Obviously these men were not about to open the academic doors of Harvard University and permit a Negro woman to earn her Ph.D. in the field of education.

As my hopes and ambitions slowly drained away, I felt the frustration of so many Negroes before and after me. I was simply the victim of the white power structure, that unassailable force which manages or mismanages our lives without risk of retaliatory blows.

Heavy of heart, I decided not to beat around the bush, yet to be polite in what I did. After all, I am a woman and a Negro, and to be polite was my family upbringing.

"Gentlemen, you are saying that to complete this research project, I must build, administer, and totally control a whole school curriculum for the entire period of the testing."

One man laughed. "So it would seem, Mrs. Browne. Even in our campus laboratory school, the third group would be an impossibility."

Then Dean Holmes said, "Mrs. Browne, you know it does take something to get a doctorate at Harvard."

"Yes, I see it does," I said.

I struggled to gain control, to put forward the personal dignity my family always expected of me. At this moment my great-grandmother, the High Priestess of my childhood, must have leaned far over the battlements of heaven to whisper to me what to say.

Before speaking up, I had no knowledge of any plan of counterattack. If I went down, and I certainly thought that I would, I knew it would be fighting. However, as a lady I prefer a rapier to a club.

"Gentlemen," I said, "I do not know whether you realize it, but I am a Rockefeller fellow, here on a grant from the General Board of Education. I think I should tell you that the General Board was not enthusiastic about my coming to Harvard University. They did not believe that Harvard University either understood the Negro teacher's needs, or had any real comprehension of the educational problems encountered in the small Southern Negro school.

"Dr. Dearborn tells me that several men from the General Board of Education, men whom I know personally from my time in Virginia, will be here next week. I hate to tell these men from the General Board, in view of their previous negative feelings about Harvard, of the decision you have reached here today. However, since I have already spent so much of the General Board's money, I feel I must now ask these men for the necessary funds to establish the type of school system you have outlined for my research project."

No one spoke.

I had let these men know that I did not stand before them alone.

I got up and left.

Unspoken, but of full knowledge on both sides of that conference table, was the fact that Harvard University, and more particularly the Graduate School of Education, had applied for a sizable grant-in-aid from the Rockefeller Foundation. The grant was for Dr. Dearborn's own pet project, the Harvard Growth Study. As I recall, the request amounted to some twelve million dollars, a not inconsequential amount of money in those depression years.

I left that conference room dry-eyed and head high, but inwardly I fled the way Haile Selassie left the Geneva Conference, absolutely crushed of spirit.

I knew the procedure. In a week to ten days I should receive a letter from the committee.

Outside Lawrence Hall, disconsolate and bitter, I stumbled along the uneven brick walks of the Harvard Yard. I had been in the "Promised Land," but my exit was at hand.

I was living in Boston with my married sister Henrietta, who would be out at that time of day. I did not want to sit home alone and brood. The Horticultural Hall had been taken over for a flower show, and I entered. This was one of those impressive harbingers of spring. Colorful beds of blooming tulips, hyacinths, daffodils, plantings of flowering crab apples had transformed the hall into a huge inside garden. There were waterfalls, plots of green grass, roses, evergreens, tropical flowers, and white-barked birch trees already in leaf.

The technique and accomplishment of man with nature was wonderful to behold. I wondered about the technique and accomplishments of man with man.

The bright and cheerful atmosphere of the flower show tore away my gloomy thoughts. Just as the organ music at Arlington Hall had refreshed my spirit, so did this promise of spring. At last I felt prepared to face Henrietta and her husband, Benny Tidball. I knew they were planning a little celebration for what was to have been my triumph.

Henrietta had absolutely no idea of what I had been through. She knew that I had been aiming for this examination. Now she sensed my lack of enthusiasm and elation, and this put a damper on our little family celebration. She had prepared one of my favorite dishes for dinner, shrimp and rice and peas. Candles flickered on the table, spread with the best tablecloth. The best of everything in that house was put before us, but my bruised heart languished in self-pity.

Henrietta probed. "I won't know until the letter comes," I told her. "A week or ten days."

"But you knew about the letter before you took the

exam," she replied. Then she said, "Rosie, remember how Papa use to say the Butlers could get the best of everybody. You are a Butler, Rose, and we don't give up."

"We all promised your father we would see you through Harvard," Benny said. "You can count on us."

Back in 1933, almost as a deathbed command, my father had called the family around him. "I want all of you to help Rosie get through that college, so she can do the great work she wants. It's the work her great-grandmother told her about. Now you help her. You hear!"

Then Henrietta brought out a box of chocolates from my husband.

Whenever my husband, who had remained with his church in Virginia, sensed that I was concerned over examinations or felt I was pushing myself too hard, he would send me a box of chocolates. He knew I would fuss over this extravagance and immediately commence worrying about the extra pounds I would be putting on. His logic reasoned that this new worry would take precedence over the old scholastic upset, and I loved him for his concern and great faith, even though I did not in this instance subscribe to his logic.

That evening the box of chocolates became the final straw. I had to excuse myself. If you must blubber, you should do it in private.

Next day I visited my faculty adviser, Dr. Dearborn. To save embarrassment about the day before, I came right to the point. I wanted to do a dry run of the first two groupings of my basic research project as originally proposed at one of the Cambridge Schools. Because I had taught there at Dr. Dearborn's request, I personally knew the principal and the curriculum supervisor.

Dr. Dearborn went with me to the Winston Street School in Cambridge and supervised the establishment of these first two groups. Although my mind and heart were starved for hope, I lost myself in my work with the poor little Italian and Irish children from the depressing poverty areas of southern Cambridge. Even in that brief time my remedial reading project developed some encouraging signs.

Dr. Dearborn visited daily. I felt sorry for him. He was under terrific pressure. I simply hadn't reacted as expected to the rebuffs of the oral examination board. And my being a Rockefeller fellow added to the problems of a difficult situation.

After he had observed my project for a week, Dr. Dearborn said, "Well, Mrs. Browne, it has some promise. It has some promise, although I still do not see how you can meet the other considerations set up by the board."

When Mr. Jackson Davis and Mr. Leo Favorot of the General Board of Education arrived at Cambridge, Dr. Dearborn arranged a luncheon meeting. These gentlemen were old friends, and I am afraid we behaved rather rudely to poor Dr. Dearborn, for we reminisced at length about Virginia and our mutual acquaintances.

Finally Dr. Dearborn brought out a transcript of my grades at Harvard University. The men from the General Board of Education congratulated me on my excellent work. While Dr. Dearborn told them about me to my face, I hardly knew I was the same person who he had previously felt could not possibly meet the oral examination board's requirements. Again, the poor man acted under great pressure.

The men from the General Board of Education had not brought to Cambridge any interim report on the status of the grant-in-aid requested by Harvard University. Also, over

standards. I cannot recall our kitchen cupboard ever containing enough plates of the same pattern to make a table setting for four. Yet, our family never sat down to a meal, but the dinner plates had been warmed in the oven. To this day my sisters warm their dinner plates, while in my home I cannot serve a cup of coffee or a bowl of soup without first placing a doily and a napkin on the table. Although poor by everyone's standards, our family aspirations and desires remained not dissimilar to those of the rich; we simply lacked the means.

My family's roots had been put down in Boston nearly fifty years before my birth. By the time my brothers and sisters and I arrived, our family had learned to shift and fend for itself in this city on the banks of the Charles River. We Butler children attended Boston's public schools, worked as domestics in its fashionable Beacon Hill homes, scoured its dock area for food bargains, its industries for steady jobs, and prayed in its churches that others might be equally blessed in this good life.

As schoolchildren we read the famous writings of New England's poets and scholars. We studied the brave deeds of New England's patriots. We listened attentively as public-school teachers told us that this American land was a land of opportunity. Although our skins were black, no one told us Butler children that the cherished American dream of equal opportunity did not include us. We believed in this American ideal, just as we cherished from day to day our simple faith that the one true God loves and cares for everyone.

This environment, Boston's cultural and civic way of life, truly helped to shape our individual lives. Yet, personal standards of performance were set and met by actions within the family.

My mother's given name was Frances. This woman had determined to give her children more out of this life than bare necessities. Besides keeping house, drilling seven children in their schoolwork, and providing us with such cultural advantages as trips to museums and free concerts and historic shrines, she was also the family's principal breadwinner.

Each morning she prepared a hot breakfast for her family. Then, before leaving for her work in a laundry and before her children left for school, my mother would organize the day's duties for each of us. There were tasks to be done before school and after school, and our mother had a favorite expression by which she informed us of our family responsibilities for that day.

"Rose," mother would say, "*I will let you* do the ironing for me tonight. And Henrietta, *I will let you* clean the stove for me."

In a real and wonderful sense our mother permitted us the favor of helping her maintain our home and family. Indeed, Mother touched each of our lives in such a manner that we were constantly warmed by her love.

My father was a self-righteous dreamer, a man of appearances but little substance. When he worked, he followed the trade of a bricklayer. However, with the first snowfall, he would draw his chair alongside the potbellied iron stove in the kitchen and wait for spring. Meanwhile, his wife and his children worked to feed and to support him.

Looking back now, I do not believe my father ever fully understood his responsibility to support his family.

With my brothers and sisters I often implored our mother, "Mother, you should leave him! He's a stinker! He's no good!"

My mother, who never raised her voice at any time, could be extremely forceful in a quiet way. "Hush, Rose!" she would say. "You blaspheme! Child, your father is an intelligent man."

This intelligent man had been expelled from Hampton Institute, Hampton Roads, Virginia, for having sponsored a petition to discontinue the third year, the year in which the Hampton student worked to pay for his first two years of schooling. Afraid to return home, my father had joined the United States Navy.

Frequently, when we children failed to show him the love and respect so freely given our mother, my father would complain, "Frances, I have seen Africa and Asia and have sailed the seven seas, yet I have never seen anything to match these kids."

My father's attitude toward his children was always bossy and dictatorial, so we learned role playing to avoid his anger. Often trapped by his own inadequacies, Father would then seek to overcome his difficulties by bringing a love offering to the family. He never personally distributed such offerings, usually candy suckers or gumdrops. Instead, pressing a bag of these treats into the hands of his favored offspring of the moment, he would say, "Now you share these with the family."

Among us, Father's favor would often shift quite suddenly from one child to another and for no apparent reason. Therefore, when a Butler child approached a family gathering bearing a love offering from our father, someone would size up the situation and say: "Look, I have fallen from grace, but when I was in paradise, I did all right by you. Now you share with me!"

My paternal grandfather died before my birth. He had been a Baptist preacher in Norfolk, Virginia. I believe my father always remembered him with genuine fear, as though his own father were only slightly less awesome than God Almighty. Although my father neither swore nor drank, after leaving home I do not believe he ever again attended a church worship service.

My paternal grandmother had remarried and lived not far from us in the city of Boston. We called her Grandma Cason, and I always considered her a social climber. If visiting was done, we went to her house.

My maternal grandfather, William Lindsey, lived in nearby Malden, Massachusetts. He was one of the joys of my childhood. I was named for his wife, Rose, and a trip to their spacious home was an event to look forward to with delightful anticipation.

Someone had obviously tampered with my grandmother Rose's family tree, for she could pass for white. She never knew for a certainty who her father was, although our family always believed it to be the white plantation owner who had been her master before the Emancipation.

Grandma Rose could recall the time, when she had been six or seven years old, that a poor white man widely known thereabouts as an illiterate drunk had died. The plantation owner sent to cabin row for my grandmother, who was so white she proved an embarrassment to the family in the big house. At the big house they dressed my grandmother in a new black dress. Next, they showed her the body of this dead white man, and told her he was her father.

My maternal great-grandmother, who lived with my grandparents at Malden, took a childish delight in shocking their occasional white visitor, such as the collector of the weekly burial insurance premium, the tax collector, or the postman. My great-grandmother would point to Grandma Rose and say to the white stranger, "Look, she's white jest like you. Her father was a white man, jest like you. Now how you suppose something like that happen?"

This maternal great-grandmother, Charlotte Ann Elizabeth Lindsey, touched my life as did no other person. She remained the greatest single influence in the lives of all members of the Butler family. To her face, we Butler children called her Grandma, but behind her back she was our beloved "High Priestess."

When we lived in Boston, our High Priestess frequently visited in our home. Later, when the death of both my grandparents forced such a decision, our High Priestess bypassed our more affluent aunts and uncles and made the happy choice to live with "Frances and the children."

All we Butler children wanted our High Priestess to live with us. She had time to spend with children. She told us stories of her earlier life. Through her graphic tales there grew before our eyes a flourishing family tree, its roots dug deep into the soil of the past and its outflung branches held high our dreams of the future. The High Priestess made us proud of this family tree, of our past heritage. She made us feel like somebody. Also, she assured us that God loved us and would care for us. We knew our future was safe. Grandma said so.

A strict disciplinarian, our High Priestess would never permit a Butler child to utter a negative remark about our parents, or let slip a slack or off-color expression. In the process of growing up we acquired a considerable respect for the flat side of her hand. We didn't mind. Usually we had it coming to us. More important, we knew that Grandma cared. She loved us, and she came with unusual proof.

"The Lord promised me my seed will never beg its bread," she told us. Although we had heard the story hundreds of times, we would implore her, "Tell it again, Grandma."

"It were back in Virginia," she would say. "I were workin' to earn one thousand dollars to buy your great-grandfather out of slavery; to make him a freedman like the Lord intended. This day I were choppin' weeds in a field of turnips. That day were so hot Hades can't be no hotter. And all the while I'm choppin', up one row of turnips and down another, this white woman was a-sittin' in the shade of her porch a-rockin' in her chair.

"My eyes stung wid sweat, my hands were blistered, my back felt broke, my arms hung broken like. At times I could hardly stand on my feet. And all the time that white woman sat a-rockin' in that cool shade.

"It was mighty hard not to hate her.

"Finally, I turned to God and begged him to save me from my small-spiritedness, to wipe away the tears from my soul. That's when He told me, the Lord did, jest as clear as I'm talking to you. He said my seed will never beg its bread."

Our High Priestess had other visions, too. I remember so well one which occurred on a winter's day when only Grandma and I were at home.

Grandma had dragged her Boston rocking chair close to

the big iron range in our kitchen. I'd helped tuck a quilt around her legs to keep out the drafts.

She sat there rocking, her chair moving to the rhythm of the hymns she hummed, sorrow songs she had first heard in Virginia. She did not sing the words, which told how the Negro endured his suffering on earth in expectation of the Gospel's promise of a reward in the hereafter. My grandma just rocked and rocked, her chair moving in time with the rhythm beat of the music she hummed.

Gradually Grandma's eyes closed and the rocker slowed and finally stood still.

It was a Saturday and I was ironing shirts. I was eleven years old at the time and I could iron shirts just like a Chinese laundryman. Although we always had a big stack of ironing at our house, I had learned to do my chores quickly. When I had done the things my mother wanted me to do, she would let me do the things I wanted to do, which usually meant reading a book.

This Saturday, when Grandma's rocker stopped and her feet stood still and her eyes closed, I thought she had dozed off.

Therefore, I was startled half to death when she spoke to me.

"Rosie!" she said. "Pass me out one of those beautiful books you're giving to the angels!"

I thought something really terrible had happened to Grandma. I would have run right out of that house, only she sat between me and the doorway.

"Grandma! Grandma! Wake up!" I shouted.

Grandma said, "Rosie, come here!"

I hesitated, but I knew better than not to do as she said.

However, I kept a respectable distance from her and started inching myself around her chair toward the back door.

"God has a great work for you to do, Rosie," my great-grandmother said. "Just now, God showed it all to me in a vision. You was passin' out big, beautiful books to the angels. But, child, you've got to give yourself to Him. Here you're eleven years old and ain't joined no church. But God wants you, Rosie. He got work for you to do. A great work with books!"

Never before had I been present when Grandma proclaimed God had spoken to her in a vision. I was absolutely terrified.

When my mother returned home from work at the laundry, I told her what had happened.

"Well, Grandma is getting old," Mother said. "But you think about what she told you. She holds great hopes for you, Grandma does. She prays over you, Rosie."

All of her life my great-grandmother kept on telling us about our heritage, about who we were, about God's promise that we would never have to beg our bread. This dear old lady, proud and fiercely independent, rallied our self-respect, set high our personal standards, and unfurled lofty ambitions for each member of our family.

People today haven't the time, nor the love in their hearts, for grandparents. We send these dear old folks to homes for the aged and wait for them to die. We begrudge them a few visits, and wait impatiently for death to claim a life that we might divide the pitiful little inheritance—while all the time, our idle grandparents could be training our children, to whom many parents give so little of their personal time.

I can't help but think that grandparents belong with their

families, in homes with children. Certainly in order to understand my family and my childhood, you first must know more about our High Priestess, my great-grandmother.

To us Butler children our High Priestess was a very important personage, unlike any other in all of south Boston. Charlotte Ann Elizabeth Lindsey was an Indian. She traced her ancestry to members of Chief Powhatan's confederacy. The Powhatan confederacy was constantly at war with the white settlers who had invaded the Indian lands in tidewater Virginia.

Finally a few years of peace ensued because of a brave act of the great chieftain's daughter, Pocahontas. This Indian princess threw herself across the body of Captain John Smith and pleaded with her all-powerful father for this white man's freedom.

When my class at the Everett public school in Boston came to this bit of history, all of Grandma's stories about the blood of Indian chieftains flowing in our family's veins came back to mind. I read and reread the several paragraphs in our history book. I loved that story of Pocahontas.

I soon insisted that all of the Butler family, and especially my brothers and sisters, call me Princess. Besides being a bit aggressive, I am also an incurable romanticist.

Few history books of that period told that Pocahontas became a Christian and in 1614 married an Englishman, John Rolfe. A few years later Pocahontas died while on a journey to England. Again continual warfare ensued between the Powhatans and the white settlers, until the settlers won a decisive battle in 1684. For all practical purposes, the great Powhatan confederacy had lost the fight for its fatherland, and to the victors went all the rich lands of a once proud and free people.

The few Indians who remained in tidewater Virginia traveled in small bands from one hunting or fishing ground to another in a futile attempt to stave off starvation and crippling disease.

In 1619 the first slave ship anchored before the square tower at Jamestown. The numbers of Negro slaves in the Old Dominion Colony increased rapidly as the plantations grew in numbers, and to a corresponding degree the opportunities for the Indians to secure occasional paying jobs diminished. Also, many white persons neither accepted nor trusted the Indian. Thus, although the Indian remained legally free under the laws of the land, his plight remained often as bad or worse than that of many Negro slaves.

Just how my great-grandmother happened to first meet Reuben Lindsey, I do not know. However, she always described our great-grandfather with such fierce pride that we knew, just as she said, the blood of African chieftains flowed in his veins. With her finger pointing at us, and her black eyes snapping us alert, our High Priestess would say, "The blood of chieftains from two continents are in the veins of you Butler children."

We were so proud.

I really do not know too many facts about Reuben Lindsey. His mother and father had been snatched from the same village in West Africa and survived the Atlantic crossing. Survival marked no small feat, as quite often but one of six black persons captured in Africa lived through the terrible Middle Passage to the New World. Most died of despair, fright, diseases, uncontrolled anger, or in valiant efforts to escape their captors. My great-grandfather's parents survived and were married in this country. So far as we know, they had but one child, Reuben Lindsey. Slave parents could be sold separately and their offspring sold away from them. My great-grandfather was a husky, intelligent lad. He undoubtedly brought a good price in the slave markets.

Reuben Lindsey was owned by Mr. Kelly Weston, whose plantation was near Deep Creek, Virginia, not far from the present city of Norfolk. Not all plantation owners were mean to their slaves, and on the word of my High Priestess, I can safely report that Mr. Kelly Weston was a good man.

However, the "marster" remained but an incidental actor to the real drama our High Priestess described to us. "Your granddaddy was a slave, but he was a house servant. He never worked a day in the fields in his whole life. He was smart. And he dressed well. Why, he wore all of Mr. Kelly Weston's old clothes, and never once had to wear no field clothes."

Obviously, even cabin row had a caste system. The house servants, picked for their intelligence and willingness to learn polite manners and to follow instructions, constituted slavery's elite and enjoyed the easiest life. At the far opposite end of slavery's caste system toiled the field hands, whose endless and exhausting labors made the plantation dollars roll in. That a young Negro man of husky build, obviously capable as a field hand, was assigned to duties as a house servant spoke eloquently of his intelligence and self-discipline, factors Grandma never permitted any of us to forget.

That Mr. Kelly Weston gave his permission for Charlotte Ann Elizabeth and his house servant Reuben Lindsey to marry was in itself remarkable. The established law of the slave states held that the children of any marriage union took the status of the mother. Therefore, in permitting his house servant to marry an Indian, a free woman, Mr. Kelly Weston lost his legal opportunity to add to his chattels through future births. (If his house servant had married a slave woman, all offspring of this marriage union would have been slaves to Mr. Kelly Weston, and their market value would have increased the financial worth of the master. Also, this law meant that the mulatto children were kept slaves, thereby denying any embarrassing legal actions seeking to share in the family inheritance of a white father.)

As further proof of his generous spirit, Mr. Kelly Weston had the marriage performed by a minister and recorded the event in a family Bible, a far cry from the usual consent of the master as "Sam and Mary took up marriage" without ceremony.

Thus, although born in Virginia in slave days, my grandfather William and my aunts and uncles were born free. However, shortly after each birth our High Priestess had to take each child to the County Court House, where the child was registered in order to secure those all-important certificates which proved that these children, her children, were free.

In later years, within the span of my memory, when Grandfather William would do something of which "Grandma" disapproved, our High Priestess would say, "I jest should have let those men sell you down the river. That's jest what I should have done."

She referred to the time when Grandfather William was three years of age. Grandma had taken little William with her when she went to Deep Creek to sell something. While negotiating her small transaction, William slipped away unnoticed. The slave-auction block was just around the corner, and in terror Grandma dashed into that crowd of white men frantically searching for her small son. Finding little William down by the slave block, Grandma clutched her child to her, and waving his papers for all to see, ran from that hated place.

It was even necessary, during the time of slavery, for a person of color to have a pass or a freedman's certificate in order to travel from one plantation to another. Anyone caught without a pass was whipped.

To discourage runaways, the masters hired poor white men, "patterolls" they were called, to patrol with bloodhounds the areas around the skirts of cabin row and the nearby towns. The patterolls armed themselves with rifle and whip, and often made use of both weapons before checking for identification papers.

Those were the papers which our High Priestess, Charlotte Ann Elizabeth Lindsey, secured for each of her children born of her marriage with Reuben Lindsey, her beloved husband, a house servant but none the less a slave.

The fact of her husband's slave status galled my greatgrandmother, but as yet she could not see clearly what she must do. When she did see, she would move with that singleness of purpose which characterized her entire life.

Both of my great-grandparents were deeply religious.

The Negro felt an inescapable sorrow over his enslavement, and in the mysticism and sacrifice of the white man's religion the black man found a release from his pent-up anguish. This in itself presented a bit of a paradox, for there were persons in the church of that day who tried to depict slavery as a manifestation of God's will.

For its text, this argument took the Great Commission: Go ye therefore, and teach all nations, baptizing them in the name of the Father, and of the Son, and of the Holy Ghost (Matthew 28:19). The meaning of this verse was willfully twisted by slavery's advocates as follows: The Great Commission is clear enough, but since we don't have enough missionaries to send overseas, we have brought the heathen to us, that we might fulfill the word of God.

Despite such hypocrisy among some white worshipers, and the slave's own anguish over his bonds, the Negro found his only sustaining hope to escape the miseries of this earth to be the Gospel's promise of a better life in the next world.

Customarily the house servants attended church with the white plantation owner's family, but in the vestibule of the church the Negroes separated and climbed up a little stairway to the balcony reserved for the colored.

The field hands seldom attended these white churches, and their own Negro preachers were few in numbers. However, under the protective shadows of evening, the house servants and the field hands would steal away into the woods, and out of sorrow and longing composed their folk hymns about their love of Jesus.

> Steal away, steal away, steal away to Jesus.
> Steal away, steal away home,
> I ain't got long to stay here.
>
> My Lord, He calls me,
> He calls me by the thunder,
> The trumpet sounds it in my soul.
> I ain't got long to stay here.

Love My Children

There was general belief in the South that Christian slaves were more responsible and less likely to run away. To have a husky young house servant, of above-average intelligence and manners, become a Christian, as was his wife, made my grandfather an increasingly valuable chattel. Yet, if the crops should fail and the plantation at Deep Creek needed ready cash, the fact that my great-grandfather was a Christian, was hard-working, and loved and cared for his family, did not mean that Mr. Kelly Weston would not hesitate to sell him down the river. Even though he had a good master, the ultimate security of Reuben Lindsey and his family could only be called precarious. Their fate depended in large measure upon the financial success of the Kelly Weston plantation.

To Charlotte Ann Elizabeth, born free and fiercely proud of it, this uncertainty became intolerable. Above all else, she wanted her husband free. Three children had blessed this marriage, and the only member of their family not free was the father. Our High Priestess vowed to change this. She would purchase Reuben Lindsey's freedom.

When she first broached this idea to her husband, he nearly panicked. He feared the consequences of even suggesting a change in the status quo. However, our High Priestess had a way of not taking No for an answer. She finally persuaded her reluctant husband to accompany her to the big house, where she asked Mr. Kelly Weston about buying her husband's freedom. Mr. Weston listened and then said he would have to think about it. Later, I do not know how much later, he sent word to Charlotte Ann Elizabeth that the release price of the bondsman, my great-grandfather, was $1,000.

It took six years for my great-grandmother to save

that much money, and during that time she bore three more children.

Most of her work was for the small truck farms nearby. She would go out into the fields in the morning and take her brood of children with her. The children would play around in the rows as she chopped weeds and tilled turnips. During the season for ripening fruit, she would pick and wrap apples and pears and small fruit and pack them in crates. In the evening she did laundry and took in sewing. Some of her income had to be used to support the family. Reuben Lindsey had no income, and could provide only the leftovers from the table and the wardrobe of the white family at the big house. However, without fail, a part of the High Priestess's cash income was set aside to buy her family their father's freedom.

The day finally came when Charlotte Ann Elizabeth and Reuben Lindsey went to Mr. Kelly Weston with the $1,000. I do not know that gentleman's reaction now that the stipulated amount of money had been raised. I do know that our High Priestess described those moments, when the master took this hard-earned money, as "prayerful moments." It was not an entirely uncommon practice for the master to take the money and refuse to release the bondsman. However, Mr. Kelly Weston kept his promise. He gave the necessary certificate to his house servant, and also had the certificate properly recorded at the County Court House.

For one person of color the chains of hated slavery had been legally broken. Mr. Reuben Lindsey was a freedman.

As man so often learns upon reaching the Promised Land of his dreams, the fruit of the Tree of Life still remains beyond his outstretched fingertips. Indeed this was the case in the life of my great-grandfather.

41

The word freedom embraces meanings and concepts set forth centuries ago in English common law, and is rooted all the way back to the common man's historic search for liberty in the days of the Greek and Roman empires. Such freedom is not a garment to be slipped on like a coat, to command visibly instant recognition and prestige. Reuben Lindsey had taken the first step through the Gates of Freedom. He was no longer the property of another man. Yet, a piece of paper pronouncing him a freedman did not alter the training of a lifetime of servitude— "hat in hand and knee bending and body bowed."

The initial days of this man's freedom proved to be a period of mounting frustration.

First the "marsters" of the neighboring plantations, whom Reuben Lindsey knew personally from his servant days at the big house of Mr. Kelly Weston, cooled in their attitude toward him. Freedmen were suspect. Freedmen were considered to be dangerous. They believed that the very presence of freedmen might put radical ideas into the heads of the disenfranchised chattels on cabin row.

As a freedman, my great-grandfather tried to assume the responsibility for the support of his family. He was ill prepared to do so, for he owned neither land, oxen, farm equipment, money, nor needed workman's skills. In the money market he competed for his daily bread against slave labor. Regardless of whether the neighboring "marsters" personally distrusted Reuben Lindsey or not, they feared his status as a freedman.

There was no work available to Reuben Lindsey, the new freedman, on any of the plantations.

Another setback was the attitude of the other colored persons. As a house servant Reuben Lindsey had held a high place in the ranks of the slaves. His had been an enviable position. However, as a freedman, someone who had managed to escape the system, he was hated.

Our High Priestess would tell us how on a Sunday, when she had dressed my grandfather William and the other children, she and her freedman husband would walk past the shacks of cabin row on their way to the only church then open to them, the bush-arbor church. They ran a gauntlet of vilification as the field hands—some idling away the time and some busy catching and cracking lice—loosened their hatreds and bitter emotions at those who had escaped from slavery.

Undoubtedly my great-grandparents and their children inflamed the situation by looking like an African version of the folks from the big house, for on Sunday they wore the hand-me-down dress clothes of the "marster and his family."

This Negro man, although a house servant, had once been a slave like them. Now he dressed as if he were somebody else. Who did he think he was?

After straightening the children's ties and skirts, my great-grandmother would line up her brood.

"Look straight ahead," she told them. "Don't you mind none what those field hands says to you. You watch your papa and your mamma and do just as we do. Hear?"

They heard.

At my birth my great-grandmother was in her late eighties, and yet I can imagine that she was quite a filly back in those Virginia days. I can just picture her, head high, each strand of her long black hair in place, her square jaw jutted forward, her white-gloved hand firm in the crook of Reuben Lindsey's arm, and the tail of her hand-me-down Paris gown just a-swishin' sassylike as she led her family to church.

They passed the witchcraft doctors, the voodoo believers, those who spitefully cried out for God's vengeance, and those who spat and cursed them with such obscenities as "Shit on a stick!"

Carefully they picked their way through the mud and the epithets and marched on, to give their thanks to the Lord.

Dark despair had replaced the first high hopes, and a persistent realization grew that as persons of color, despite freedman status, theirs remained a reenslavement in this land of slavery. This terrible truth fretted my great-grandmother. It revealed again an outcropping of her unyielding determination, a stubborn vein of family character which despite all odds would admit no defeat. Yet, our High Priestess was never too proud to recognize that a different approach might be more practical.

Under the light of this new revelation her thoughts continued to dwell upon freedom.

I remember as a little girl sitting on the lap of my High Priestess as she explained how she had tried to encourage Reuben Lindsey to act like a freedman. "He just couldn't get over bein' no ex-slave," she would say. "He'd pass a white man in the street and he'd get off the sidewalk, like colored folks down South has to do, but he still looks down to the toes of his shoes. He don't look that white man in the eye, eye to eye, like he's a freedman and he knows it. I tells him he don't have to look down for no man, white or colored. He's free! All he has to do is be polite. That's what I tried to teach your great-grandfather."

However, half a lifetime in slavery and a man's habits

become a part of him—as though they were a physical part of his person. Although the blood of chieftains of Mother Africa ran in his veins, Reuben Lindsey could not rid his mind of slavery's chains by the mere possession of his freedman certificate.

The realization that her family possessed pieces of paper but not freedom, and her so painful awareness that the spirit of freedom cannot be purchased, failed to lessen my great-grandmother's hope to attain her goal—freedom for her children.

Now she clearly understood what she must do, and she obviously had the courage to give to this dream. I do not believe she ever knew that she was supposed to be inferior. She felt herself superior to most, and she probably was closer to the truth than many people of different social strata who detracted her.

In this year of 1848 the dock area of Norfolk was bordered by giant boxlike warehouses. These buildings were separated one from another by muddy streets. Through these streets the straining horses, heavily laden wagons, and swearing drovers made slow but noisy progress. The docks themselves were piled high with the harvest of raw products from the fertile Virginia soil and the enslaved blackman's ceaseless labors.

On another part of the docks stood stacked boxes of manufactured goods, elegantly styled clothes and household goods from European capitals. These symbols of wealth would be purchased by Virginia's few persons of means, admired by those who coveted wealth, but would never be available to the black persons whose labor had produced the wealth which made this commerce possible.

Picking her way through the mud and traffic of the

crowded streets of the dock area came this pride-powered lady of color. In one arm she held my great-aunt Romelia, then not yet a year old, while her other hand had a locklike grip on the hand of my great-aunt Laura, who was then just past her third birthday. However, her concern was for my beloved grandfather William, a sturdy five-year-old, who vainly tried to keep up by hanging on to her full skirts with both his tiny hands.

Head high, glancing neither to right nor left, my great-grandmother went straight ahead. However, the children, and especially little William, looked about in amazement, sometimes shivering in fright and again in awe and bewilderment.

Many strong young Negro slaves were at work at the docks, their muscular backs bent beneath the loads they carried. They chanted one of the sorrow songs, timing their steps to the slow rhythm of the music. As these stevedores moved to their assigned tasks, the whites of their eyes showed as they watched their overseers without appearing to do so.

At sight of this colored lady and her three children, the black stevedores and their white overseers watched in surprise. Charlotte Ann Elizabeth Lindsey ignored them. She made inquiry of several sailors until she was certain of the boat, and then, without a backward glance, she carried and half dragged her three children up that gangplank.

I suppose it was the ship's captain who was summoned. He demanded to see her papers. Convinced that this colored woman's papers were in proper order for herself and these three children, he told her the price for steerage passage to Boston.

With a laugh he turned his head while my great-grandmother, from beneath the folds of her dress and petticoats, retrieved the passage money.

The captain called for a seaman.

"Show these Nigars to the bottom," he said.

No family member could take off work that day to come to the dock. Family farewells had already been made. In this land where one had to become accustomed to seeing loved ones and friends "sold down the river," partings were a way of life, not welcome but tolerated.

My great-grandmother had determined to leave this land of her birth, the fatherland of her once proud race. She was also leaving behind her not quite so bold but greatly beloved husband. Reuben Lindsey lacked the courage to venture farther down freedom's road. Unable to make it on his own, he was back working as a house servant for Mr. Kelly Weston, sleeping in and drawing a meager pay.

In this land she both loved and hated, our High Priestess also left a married daughter who had borne her first grandchild. This married daughter, Marliene, would care for the two older Lindsey children, both in their teens, who could now work to support themselves.

These older members of her family would care for one another and manage to exist, as colored people had done before, but for the younger members of her family this determined lady held high hopes. These children would grow up in freedom.

Down the ship's companionways they followed the sailor, past smoking lanterns and down narrow stairs. No words were spoken. The children clung to their mother. As she walked, this High Priestess of our family silently prayed, "Lord, thanking ye that these young 'uns is going to have freedom. We's trusting in your promise, Lord, that my seed won't ever have to beg no bread. You been good to us, Lord. Thank ye."

The sailor left them in the dim-lit steerage compartment. In one corner she put down the baby, a welcome signal for the other two children to let go of their mother. They watched and whimpered softly as their mother worked the circulation back into her numb arms.

In the dim light, Charlotte Ann Elizabeth could see that her children were frightened. So she gathered the little ones between her knees, and resting her back against the wooden sides of the ship, she sang to her children the sorrow songs of the slave.

Perhaps the melody had a heathen origin and had been brought over from Africa on the slave ships. However, the words were Afro-American, the cry of an unhappy people unafraid of death and wearied by their labors, who expressed a longing for a truer and happier world.

> Dust, dust and ashes, fly over my grave,
> But the Lord shall bear my spirit home.

She might not have sung this particular song, but one like it. I know that she sang of her Lord Jesus, for I never knew my great-grandmother to sing a purely secular song.

When the children had stopped whimpering, she pulled from the pack which had been tied around her back a rag blanket for each child. Taking a gourd drinking cup from the pack, she drew water from a cask that sat on the floor in the middle of the steerage compartment, next to the giant pole of the mast, which extended both above and below this compartment area. She passed the water-filled gourd to each child and herself drank the remaining contents. She gave each child a hard biscuit; this simple fare was their supper.

Other steerage passengers, most of them white, had entered the compartment and took floor space opposite my great-grandmother.

The children soon fell asleep, but Charlotte Ann Elizabeth did not close her eyes. Beneath the folds of her dress she had hidden the papers which proclaimed their freedom status, despite their color. She dared not sleep until the ship passed safely out of port, lest someone take those papers from her.

Thus she lay awake, in a half-sitting position against the ship's side, when the sails were hoisted. She heard the creaking of the canvas and halyards and felt the vibration of the ship moving through the water. The city of Norfolk fell astern, and they passed Hampton Roads. As the ship entered the channel of Chesapeake Bay and headed for the tip of Cape Henry, the last bit of Virginia soil to be passed, she maintained her vigil. Her thoughts dwelt not on Virginia but on freedom. Her prayers were not for herself but for her children.

"Lord, you leadin' 'em to freedom! Thank ye, Lord."

With her three smallest children, my great-grandmother was on her way to Boston. She knew no one in Boston. She had absolutely no knowledge of the city of Boston, other than that it was the center of the Abolitionist Movement. This movement called for the freedom of the slave on the grounds that slavery was not morally right. At least that is what the rumors around the plantations' cabin rows in northern Virginia had said. When folks take such a bold stand, my great-grandmother reasoned, they must love freedom and those whom they wish to set free. Rumor had it that most Abolitionists were preachers and lawyers. Certainly these good men would welcome this original American in search of freedom for her three very small children.

If my great-grandmother's knowledge of the Abolitionists was somewhat sketchy, her faith in God never faltered. God had provided miracles in her life. He would not forsake her now.

The passage to Boston on this coastal schooner took nearly a week. The nausea of seasickness did not last long, but the boredom of steerage passage, the atmosphere of the dark and smelly quarters took their toll. The children became cross and irritable.

Later our High Priestess often told us how she had marched to freedom up that gangplank at Norfolk, the three tiny children clinging to her. But to my recollection she never described how they had disembarked at Boston, nor did she tell us of her initial reactions to this citadel of American freedom and faith, this new home which she had chosen.

These pitifully poor arrivals must have created a forlorn, even ludicrous, sight there on the docks of Boston: a forty-year-old Indian woman with three tiny waifs so dependent and trusting. Their clothing, suitable for Virginia's cabin row, must have appeared uncouth; while their slurred accents and colloquial words must have had a strange sound amid the down-east accents familiar in this New England port. Yet these travelers' hearts were human and their plight ageless.

My grandfather William once told me that when they came ashore in Boston they were cold and hungry. He said they had been turned away at lodging houses and sneered at in cafés.

This must have been a disheartening experience for my proud great-grandmother.

I imagine she pushed right on from one rebuff to another until her children needed to rest. She found them a public bench where they might sit while she prayed and sang to them.

One of the best things about Negro people, poor as we still are, is our sense of compassion for anyone whose heart is filled with the awful pain that only man can afflict on his fellow man. Thus it happened that a Negro woman passing that public bench overheard the words and recognized the melody of great-grandmother's sorrow song. She saw one of God's children in need of love, and she spoke to my great-grandmother. This woman had come from Virginia, via the Underground Railway, and she knew the loneliness of a great city. Although she had little more than a roof over her own head, for herself and her family, she took in these four strangers.

Thus Charlotte Ann Elizabeth Lindsey and her three children moved in with another family, like 'possums, and survived.

I have never known for a certainty where my family lived those first few months in Boston. From hearing my grandfather William's description, their quarters (for more than a dozen persons) must have been a loft room beneath the roof of some large warehouse building not far from the Boston docks. The loft made quite an impression on William. In Virginia he had looked out the front doorway of their cabin to the flatness of the open fields stretching wide before him. Now, with nose pressed against a windowpane (itself a novelty), he looked down, down, down to the street below. The street was crowded with horses and wagons; "looking like ants" is how my grandather William described the scene.

Everything in Boston appeared crowded to these rural immigrants. William and the younger children did not like to leave the loft. They drew back from the noisy, jostling crowds on the sidewalks below, from the great rumbling wagons in the streets. The people themselves frightened the children. Nearly everyone in Boston was white, and they spoke differently from the whites in Virginia. Back in Deep Creek the whites had not been so numerous, but they had been people to fear. Even the good whites like Mr. Weston were feared. Here nearly everyone was white, and of the children William at least was frightened.

Charlotte Ann Elizabeth realized that despite their tender ages she had brought her children out of Virginia none too soon. She prayed that the freedom she sought might be revealed to her here in Boston, in God's good time.

My great-grandmother managed to find a job scrubbing floors. The work appeared ideal for her at the time. She could be with her children during the daytime, and the Negro family that had befriended them gave her children their evening meal and put them to bed. Thus Charlotte Ann Elizabeth started a new life, mothering her children, being their breadwinner in the city of Boston.

All this she tolerated for freedom.

Chapter 3

THE MELTING POT

When I was a child, my grandparents' home in Malden, Massachusetts, just outside Boston, was my favorite place. It was a large two-story frame dwelling of typical plain New England architecture, surrounded on three sides by a covered piazza. The house stood on a spacious corner lot, and in this yard Grandfather tended his peach and apple trees and grew some delicious grapes. He always said no one was too poor to raise a pig or plant a garden.

My grandparents' home was always there, always the same. It had a big entrance hall, to the right of which there were double doors which opened into a double parlor furnished in horsehair furniture that scratched your legs as you climbed up on a chair.

Beyond the double parlors was the dining room, where a huge stove was burning in the wintertime. Next came the kitchen. From the kitchen there was a small entryway which led to the bathroom—with its zinc-lined bathtub, washbowl, and commode—and on out to the yard.

The kitchen had a big pantry full of good-smelling things: spices, cookies, gingerbread, syrup, fresh-baked bread, and all the things children liked. There was also a huge wooden icebox, lined with zinc, which had four big doors. One door was for the ice compartment, another for the meat which Grandpa William salted and packed in there every week until the door would hardly close. One of the two lower compartments held Grandma Rose's currently prepared food, and the other her butter, eggs, and buttermilk. The center piece of furniture in the kitchen, of course, was the huge kitchen range.

Upstairs were five bedrooms—four large ones and a small one over the front hall. In Grandma's room there was a chest full of quilts, afghans, and sheets, pillowcases, and clean rags for a sick day. Drawers held unbleached cotton sheets for everyday use. Grandma's bed was high with mattresses, and it had a bolster covered with pillow shams. You hardly dared touch her bed, and sitting on it was impossible. Grandpa's room upstairs was finally abandoned because his rheumatism was aggravated by climbing the stairs. He slept in the back parlor on a daybed. Now that the children were all married and had left home, the other bedrooms were used for company or for "Frances and the children" when Mother brought us to this wonderful house.

The parlors were filled with oval-framed tintypes of the family. Most of my relatives, it seemed, were very good-looking women with Indian features, who wore gold beads around their necks. The faces always smiled, and the eyes seemed to follow you everywhere you moved in that room.

Although Grandfather told me the names of these ancestors and all about them, I seldom listened carefully. After all, I knew only our immediate family circle, while almost all of my great-grandmother's family were dead; but I was fearful of the sneaky way in which they watched me.

The reason I so loved to be at my grandparents' house was that my father, whenever he found a job as a bricklayer, liked to move to be near where he was working. When he worked, we moved. For us Butler children moving meant making new friends and changing schools. I do not recall that I ever went more than two years to the same school. Yet we never moved away from the south end of Boston, where the newly arrived immigrants lived.

Despite this constant changing of residence, our sense of personal pride and family loyalty and our mother's sweet love soon made of each new home an island of security. And my great-grandmother's glowing pride and fierce love made us feel forever challenged. We would not have exchanged our humble home for life in the finest residence on Boston's elegant Beacon Hill.

At this time there were no restrictions on immigration to America. Boston's South End population was largely first-generation Irish, newly arrived Italians, newly arrived Russians, some German Jews, and some Negroes. My High Priestess never let us forget that there were four generations of our family living in Boston, and that she had lived in Massachusetts more than fifty years.

However, we merged into the melting pot and took on the cultures that were a part of group living. When Hymie had to go to the synagogue on Saturday to learn Hebrew, to study the Torah, and to prepare for his Bar Mitzvah, my brother hurried to do his chores and be free to play when

Hymie came home. When Patrick and Annie O'Malley went
to say the Stations of the Cross, we went too. At first we
waited outside, then we went inside very quietly and waited,
but later we learned to kneel at each picture and make the
Stations. We did not tell our parents because we feared that
they might not understand. I know that my High Priestess
would have predicted that God was going to send a big judgment on us.

When Mrs. McSweeney had a new baby, my mother sent
me with a pitcher of gruel to help bring her milk so that she
could nurse her baby. When Alice Donohue took her first
communion, she wore the very beautiful dress that my
Aunt Lill had made my sister Mary for a children's day
program. When I went to Winning Farm, the camp which
the Morgan Memorial Church ran for poor children in
Hopkinton, Massachusetts, and later at South Athol, I
wore the camp togs that a neighbor girl had used at the
Young Women's Hebrew Association camp.

When the High Holy Days of the Jewish families came,
we shared in the feasting. Also, we made money lighting fires
on Saturday mornings because after sunset on Friday, Ortho-
dox Jews did no work until their Sabbath was over at sunset
on Saturday.

In those days the national origin of the members of this
melting pot was of no consequence. Family concern for other
families, the desire of all to rear good and respectful children made us children realize that all of the parents were together on what was right and decent. When Mr. Fischel
David, a respected Jewish neighbor, came to our door and
said, "Mr. Butler, your children threw rocks at my horse,"
my father said, "Thank you, Mr. David." Then we said,

"May we go to bed now? We don't feel so good!" We knew we had done wrong.

Surrounded by the diverse cultures in this melting pot, we Butlers never doubted that we were going places. We had firm guidance. No choice existed to take either the high road or the low road. In our family you took the high road, or else. The miracle of our mother's love bound us together, and even our father, just by being there, strengthened our feeling of security: We were a whole family.

My mother was elated when she had her first daughter. My two brothers were my seniors by four and eight years, respectively, but poor Mother did not know that four more little girls would soon follow. Yet, I doubt this practical woman ever deceived herself that the family's support would be anyone's burden but hers.

Naturally, persons outside the family touched our lives, some in wonderful ways, but our guidance and all the responsibility which that entails fell on two dear women, my mother and my High Priestess. They accepted the burden without fanfare or fear. The Lord so privileged it, and they loved their God.

My birth necessitated Mother's closely scheduling her time. Each Butler child first met her planned program in the matter of the bath. Buckets of water stood heating on top of the huge kitchen range while we ate supper. After the evening meal, a galvanized iron tub was dragged in front of the big stove, close by its reflected warmth. The tub was then filled with water and tempered to the right temperature.

With wash rag and soap and towel, Mother was ready.

A firm believer in the Good Book and in the good effects

of soap and water, Mother attacked each of us Butler children with a vigorous conviction that cleanliness was next to godliness. She made our blackness shine, and in the process convinced each of us that we should take our own baths. This usually occurred before the third birthday. Although we knew we had to pass Mother's rigid inspection, we suffered that risk in preference to having our hides rubbed off as she scrubbed and toweled us dry.

Unknown to us, our education in family living had started.

While you were being bathed, your underclothes were soaking in the same tub and then were washed and hung on the inside clothesline stretched behind the kitchen stove. Your outer clothes went into the regular laundry, to be rubbed clean on a scrubboard in the laundry tub and then hung on the outside line. Often in those New England winters these outer garments, when brought inside, had to be hung on the inside line to thaw, for they would be frozen into stiff, grotesque shapes.

When your bath and chores were finished, Mother would dip out half the bath water, add fresh water, and beckon to the next child.

The decision to take over my own bath was hastened by the arrival of our sister Mary, who in three years was followed by the arrival of our sister Henrietta. Between having babies, Mother continued working at the laundry. Father, aided part of the time by our Aunt Lill or our High Priestess, baby-sat. Sometimes, in good weather, Father's work opened up. Meanwhile, Mother's five-and-a-half-day week at the laundry and the money my two brothers contributed from their newspaper routes supported our family.

On Sunday, that day of rest, our weekly routine was broken in one of two ways.

When no family gathering had been planned, we often took the Belt Line trolley, a five-cent car ride that carried you around the city of Boston and brought you back to your starting point. Sometimes, if we didn't have enough nickels for all, we would walk with our mother to the Museum of Fine Arts, to the Boston Common, or to the Boston Public Garden. We loved to sit on the grass in the Public Garden and watch the swan boats on the lagoon, and when we tired of that, watch the hurrying people.

At other times we would just walk, from one end of Boston to the other, and look at the buildings and historic sites known today as tourist attractions. We visited Paul Revere's house, both old North and South Churches, and we were at Bunker Hill for Patriot's Day (then the big spring-time event in Boston). Here I became so fascinated at seeing men dressed as redcoats and carrying old muskets that I got lost.

We also visited Longfellow's Home, along with the homes of the other New England intellectuals and writers, and even traveled to historic Lexington and Concord.

If there was a free concert at the Charles River Basin, we were there. If there was a lecture at the Museum of Fine Arts, we were there. Mother, who had had but two years of high school education, but had lived all her life in Boston, had an absolute obsession that every cultural advantage must be utilized for her children. She never doubted that we were ready for such cultural exposure.

In those days a wonderful column appeared in the Boston *Daily Globe* under the heading "The Housekeeper's Column" (now known as the "Confidential Chat"). This column contained recipes and ways of stretching food for children. It also told of new books recommended for children. In picturesque language, it described winters along the sandy exposure of Cape Cod or in the wooded Berkshire Hills. Every day it listed the free concerts and lectures in the central Boston area. Mother never missed this column, and it was almost the total extent of her reading.

My father read a great deal—*Collier's, The Saturday Evening Post.* Light and current reading appealed to him, but I do not recall that he ever once joined the family on one of those cultural trips.

Naturally, before starting these outings, we had been to church. Mother insisted we attend white churches "because you learn more in a white church." So, although Charlotte Ann Elizabeth rode the trolley seven miles each Sunday to attend the Twelfth Baptist Church, the Boston church for Negro Baptists of that day, we attended Sunday school and church in nearby neighborhood churches with primarily white congregations.

I do not recall that we ever had any misunderstandings with our fellow church members.

Our other Sabbath diversion was a family gathering for Sunday dinner at my grandfather William's house in Malden, an occasion even my father did not miss.

It was an exciting trip. We would ride the streetcar to Sullivan Square or the elevated train to the Dover Street Station, and then the surface trolley to Malden. The address was 3 Sammett Street.

En route we frequently met the High Priestess on her way home from the Twelfth Baptist Church. She was tall and broad-shouldered and sure-footed and just noble in her stature and her appearance. Her complexion glowed red-brown in color, beneath black straight hair that became gray at the temples only after she had passed her ninetieth birthday.

She took great pride in her appearance, our High Priestess. She would affix little bunches of velvet violets to her hats for Sunday and wear a black blouse with a white ruching at the neck. Beneath her full skirt were several taffeta petticoats which swished to her rapid stride. On communion Sundays she stayed for the evening-worship service and returned to Malden on the streetcar late at night by herself.

My brother John said the Malden streetcar looked deserted after the Butler family got off; often more than fifty persons gathered for those Sunday dinners.

By the time we arrived, Grandma Rose would have the dining room ready. The table had an oilcloth cover, but no table spread with the finest damask cloth and sterling-silver place sets was more properly arranged. There would be a centerpiece of homegrown flowers, a bowl of fresh fruit and nuts in season, and candlesticks. No matter if the water glasses had once contained jelly, for all of us children knew that no poor people could ever hope to have such a feast.

The children were served first. There would be platters of roast beef and of fried chicken, dishes of vegetables, plates of hot breads, and a wooden tub of delicious homemade butter.

And always there was gingerbread.

Grandfather William worked at Gould's Herb Factory, on the Mystic River upriver from Malden, and there always remained about his person the rich, pungent aroma of herbs. On his table there always stood plates of rich dark gingerbread. Grandfather's gingerbread was distinctive. It undoubtedly was the gingeriest of all gingerbreads, the kind that tickles the nose and brings tears to the eyes, but it was delicious.

Grandfather William said grace twice—first for the children's meal, and then for the adults. His was not the traditional mealtime prayer, but an expression of thankfulness for all those who had recently done something kind to him or to a member of his beloved family. It was a poem of praise for the godly in man.

My grandfather was devoted to my mother, his oldest daughter, but he never thought much of my father. With his own children married now, Grandfather felt that he should help care for his daughter and her children.

His attention had been given to my older brothers before me, and I could hardly wait until I had reached the first grade and was considered old enough to go alone to Malden on Fridays after school. Then I could sit down in that wonderful house and eat dinner with my grandparents and our High Priestess and spend the night with them.

Saturday morning my grandfather would arise early and go to work at the herb factory. After finishing the chores at the Sammett Street house, I would bid Grandmother and my High Priestess good-bye and take the trolley car to Boston to meet Grandfather William at 1 :00 P.M. in the wholesale food markets in the Dock Square area. I would bring along a market basket, and we would go shopping. My grandfather would buy entirely too much for three old people. Finally grandfather would open the stiff butcher's wrapping paper, divide the purchases, and rewrap them. For the Butlers there would be ten pounds of spareribs, a huge roast, or some other delicacy he knew we could never afford. Then he would give me a nickel to ride the subway home.

Of course I saved the nickel so I would have carfare for

the Belt Line streetcar the next day. This meant I hitched a ride home on any wagon going in my direction. If it happened to be an oat wagon, I would be covered with oats, or whatever the contents of the wagon, but I saved my nickel and held on tightly to those wonderful packages of meat. I was so proud when I arrived home with my grandparent's gifts.

However, as the Butler family increased, even Grandfather William's assistance could not meet the unflagging demand of our necessity. That is when a neighbor told Mother about "The Place." The Place was located in Pie Alley in the theatrical district off Copley Square. Specifically it was the back of a hotel, the name of which I have forgotten.

You brought a market basket to The Place, with an identifying ribbon on the handle. At a given time a man would open the back door and take in all the baskets of the poor people waiting there in the alley. In about an hour he would bring the baskets back. As he held aloft each basket for identification, you would come forward to claim your basket and pay the man a dime.

In the basket would be crusts of bread, cut off from sandwiches, and the ends of all kinds of meat that had become too small to stay in holders. Most of the time the man gave us just bread and meat for the small fee.

Often I went with my mother to The Place and we would take the basket right home and make soup, or hash, or bread pudding, and all kinds of tasty things. My mother was a good cook, and she was ingenious. From the column in the Boston *Daily Globe* she got wonderful ideas on how to stretch the food. She kept a scrapbook of recipes.

Eventually we made two main dishes with ingredients

from The Place. One we called American Chop Suey. We'd grind up the meat and put rice, spaghetti, tomatoes, onions, celery, and spices into it. It made a big pot of food so delicious we would all eat and eat until our stomachs hurt. The other main dish was potato and ground-meat hash, which we ate with our baked beans on Saturday afternoon. On Sunday we had fish cakes and beans. We never knew hunger, though we were not subsidized and told we were poor. We simply used our brains and did the best with what we had.

Of course, not all of our diversions occurred on the weekend. In nice weather we were sure to have a hurdy-gurdy man come by and entertain us. Most hurdy-gurdy men were from Italy and still felt insecure in the English language. These recent immigrants would purchase or rent a music box and then wander the streets playing and singing for a few pennies. Most often the hurdy-gurdy man himself passed around his tin cup, but sometimes he had a little monkey on a leash who did it for him. That was most exciting of all.

When the hurdy-gurdy man would play his music box and sing, all the children in the neighborhood would come running. We would dance on the sidewalks. It didn't matter if you danced with another girl, because the boys were usually too shy to dance. Anyhow, we were just dancing and singing for joy. When the hurdy-gurdy man had finished playing in front of our house and went down the street, all the children would follow him as far as they were permitted to go. Every time he stopped and played and sang, we stopped and sang and danced.

Often in Boston the hurdy-gurdy man would not be the only person in the gathering of children who felt insecure with the English language. But no bother! The music box, the Italian operatic arias, the songs and the dancing and the smiling faces were communication enough. Everyone was welcome. Everyone was having fun.

Another warm-weather visitor was the hokeypokey man who came around selling ice-cream cones. In his little wagon were many jars of various colored juices for his ice cream. For a penny you got a little cone with some sticky juice on top of the ice cream. For two cents you got a larger cone.

When the hokeypokey man came around his hoarse voice announced his approach, for he hollered, "Hokeypokey! One penny! Two penny! Hokeypokey! Come get your hokeypokey!"

If we had one or two pennies we'd run out and buy an ice-cream cone and sit on the curb with friends and lick it slowly to make the ice cream last a long, long time.

We learned early at the Butler house that if you wished to do things with the other children, like attend the Saturday matinee at the nickelodeon, you must earn your own money. I scrubbed floors, washed, ironed, and did whatever my mother directed me to do to earn a dime for the matinee. Admission was one nickel and the other nickel was for a huge bag of molasses kisses.

At these early movies I saw *Little Eva* and wept copiously, so deep was my vicarious suffering. *The Perils of Pauline* half frightened me to death. In between reels, the song leader would come on stage and lead us in singing while the house lights were turned on. The singing was wonderful. Everyone sang! There existed a feeling of kinship between audience and song leader, and we harmonized joyfully regardless of our racial and nationality backgrounds. This was America, and the harmonizing was all that mattered.

Many a cold night we Butler children sat around the kitchen stove and sang these same songs first learned at the nickelodeon. Our brother John appointed himself the song leader. Everyone suggested his favorite songs, but John had a habit of accepting only those songs he wanted to sing. This led to loud arguments when John persistently left out your song. The outcry would bring one of our parents, usually Father, to the kitchen.

"Now what's the matter?" Father would demand.

Often I was the loudmouth making the trouble, so I'd say, "Papa, John won't sing any of my songs. He just sings the songs he wants. But he won't sing one of mine."

My father would remove his glasses and shake his head as though this constant juvenile bickering were too much for him. "Now John, you go around in a circle and let everyone select a song. That's fair! You hear? I don't want to have any more fussing."

When Papa left, John and I would make a few faces at each other, being careful not to complain out loud. We didn't want "old Butinsky," as we sometimes called Father, to make a second trip to the kitchen.

Before going to bed Mother often made us some cocoa, and sometimes gave us a slice of bread with Karo syrup on it. This was a party! We had a wonderful time eating ordinary coarse food and singing. We found kinship of spirit as well as kinship of blood.

I often think about those nights. Nothing cost money. We would try to create for ourselves ways of having fun, ways to enjoy ourselves. We knew that we had to do things of which our parents approved, yet we learned how to whisper and talk in undertones of those things we knew our parents would not approve.

Whenever it became too quiet in the kitchen, one of our parents would say, "What are you all doing?"

Of course, everyone would answer, "Nothing!"

The fact that we always stuck together gave us the protection so necessary for survival.

For instance, when we went out in the evening, we were always sent in pairs. As soon as we got away from the house we might split up and go our own separate ways, but we would wait at the appointed place for the other member to show up before we returned home. No one was going to spoil the good life for the others, even if it meant standing outside under a street light in a cold New England rain while waiting for a tardy brother or sister.

There was another remarkable thing about our childhood home. We had work standards. As Charlotte Ann Elizabeth said, "Only that which you earn has real lasting value." We were taught to take pride in what we did.

I can remember scrubbing the floor and looking up at my High Priestess and saying, "Grandma, how's my floor?"

Grandma might reply, "I can see a streak."

She wasn't worried about hurting my feelings or giving me a complex. She told me the truth. My work wasn't up to standard.

The accolade we all sought from her was, "That's pretty good!" I never remember her saying, "That's good!"

I suppose all people have to be taught to live in a family group. We were. In the face of our petty disagreements, my despairing mother used to say, "Little birds in a nest must agree."

In turn we would say, "You're my sister, so you've got to agree with me."

The problem was that the big birds always pushed the little birds out of the nest and made them fly.

I started flying when I went to public grade school. Nature

simply does not permit a vacuum, so if young heads are not filled with culture and education and learning and love, other and possibly less desirable items will fill that cranium space. I was indeed ready for school.

I went to kindergarten at the Rice Training School (a branch of Boston Normal) at the corner of Appleton and Dartmouth Streets in the heart of Boston.

The first day was one of some note. Mother brought me and left me in the hall with the Admissions Clerk. I was all eyes. I knew that I was someone important now. My older brothers went to school. My two baby sisters at home did not go to school. Unnoticed I wandered through the school and on outside. I wanted to see what the world looked like. I walked several blocks to where I could look down the street and see Copley Square, before realizing that if I went any farther I would surely get lost. At least I had that much sense. However, with a small child's failure to understand time, it seemed that I had been away from home all day. Instead of returning to school, I went home. Mother was just leaving for the laundry. I had been gone all of forty-five minutes. In those forty-five minutes I had learned that the world is a great deal larger than I had imagined.

At kindergarten we were taught to go to a policeman if lost and to tell him our name and address. Thus I knew what to do when I got lost at the Battle of Bunker Hill monument on Patriot's Day. We also had parades and gala festivities on St. Patrick's Day, which was also Evacuation Day, the day the British lifted the siege of Boston.

However, of my kindergarten I remember most of all Valentine's Day. We were making valentines to take home to our mothers. Each child made a valentine place mat and then the teacher gave us two gummed angel heads to paste down on our valentine mat. The teacher gave me two heads which both faced the same direction. I could see that other children had angel heads which faced different directions. I asked the teacher for an angel head which faced the other direction.

The teacher said, "You'll take those or none!"

In my actions to placate my father, I had learned to talk under my breath and angrily said, but so low that the teacher didn't hear me, "You stinker!"

Then I explained that I wanted to give back one head for one facing the other direction, so it would not take any more heads to fulfill my simple request.

The teacher shook her head and moved on impatiently.

To me (and this is one of the little nuances some of my people today fail to notice) there was nothing racial about this act. This teacher had not replied to my request in a kind tone, for she simply was not a kind teacher. She had a mean disposition and was not the type of person who should be a teacher of children. There is a marked difference between incompetence and racial antagonism.

It was the following year, while I attended the first grade at the Fayette Street School, that little Thelma was born. This was the year that Mother left Father. We moved to Grandfather William's house in Malden, where I attended the Cross Street School.

I have mentioned that my father's inability to provide for his family distressed my grandfather William, who had become increasingly alarmed at the rate little girls were being added to the Butler family. Of those months at Malden, I remember most of all my High Priestess arguing with my mother. "Frances, those children won't amount to nothin'

69

long as all they got is their own labor, an' them trained fer only the cheapest kind of labor."

I knew I had to do better. My great-grandma had said so.

I developed into a good reader that year, although I remember an example which clearly shows how backward were the educational concepts of that day. I was reading aloud the story about the City Mouse and the Country Mouse. My problem was a misconception of the word "city," which I mistook for a form of the verb "to sit." Therefore, what I was reading did not make sense to me, so I stopped reading.

"What's the matter, Rose?" the teacher asked. "You read very well."

Finally I asked what the country mouse was doing while the city mouse was sitting.

The teacher of course laughed and was greatly amused.

In those days it was assumed that if you could pronounce the word, if you could just say the word, you understood it. Of course, educators now know this is entirely wrong. The point is, it simply was not in this teacher's kit of skills to help her pupils acquire concepts or meanings of words. If this teacher had known better she would have helped me, for she was a conscientious teacher.

By the time I started second grade, the Butler family had been reunited, Mother was soon pregnant again, and I attended first the Rutland Street School for two years and then the Everett School.

I had a delightful middle-aged second-grade teacher, a large stout woman possessed of much love and good humor. One day a terrible thunderstorm disturbed our class period. I remembered my High Priestess saying that when the Lord was busy talking you didn't talk or disturb Him. Here was

an instance of my great-grandmother's adherence to super-
stition, but of course I didn't know that at the time.

Obviously, Mrs. Vial, the teacher, had not heard my
great-grandmother's statement. Very properly, she tried to
keep her pupils calm by talking above the noise of the storm.
When she called on me to answer a question, I was in a
dilemma. My High Priestess had instructed me to keep
quiet during such a storm or I would anger the Lord. I
wasn't nearly as afraid of angering the Lord as I was of my
High Priestess, whom I had no intention of angering.

I ran to Mrs. Vial and buried my head in her ample bosom,
and the dear lady thought me terrified by the storm and running to her for protection. Fortunately she did not ask me
the reason for my actions. That would have made it necessary for me to tell her that I was doing what my grandma
had told me to do, keep quiet.

It was during my third grade that many, many events
happened to our family. The most tragic was the death of my
grandmother Rose. I went to the funeral. I was heartbroken.
Although Charlotte Ann Elizabeth still lived with her son,
my grandfather William, and they occasionally again held
family dinners, those Sunday dinners never again reached
the peak of excitement previously enjoyed. Gradually the
dinners stopped, and if Charlotte Ann Elizabeth wanted to
stay over from the morning to the evening services of the
Twelfth Baptist Church, she rested at our house.

Also, our High Priestess spent a great deal of time at our
house, almost as much as she did at Malden.

This same year my grandma taught me a most important
lesson of politely defending one's own rights, something every
Negro American must learn.

I had our High Priestess' pride and independent spirit.

We Butlers were somebody, and we were going to be somebody even more important. I knew this! My High Priestess said so, and the Lord had told her.

One day my teacher stopped me as I strutted around the classroom as if I owned the whole schoolhouse, and told me to behave myself.

I went home and told Grandma what my teacher had said. My High Priestess pulled me over to her lap.

"Rosie," she said, "you go back to that school and tell that white woman your grandma says that you're supposed to strut around and hold your head up in the air until you do something yourself to make it drop. You understand me, Rosie. Now you go tell her!"

Then I heard her say, as she did in times of extremity, "My Lord, My God! Jesus, Master!" I knew then that I had better do just as the High Priestess said.

Next day I told my teacher just what my Grandma had told me to say.

The teacher only said, "Sit down, Rose." So I sat down.

The Rutland Street School was an almost completely white school, a fact I did not notice at the time. Those were the days when playgrounds were divided, so at recess time the boys were on one side and the girls on the other side of the dividing fence. I have mentioned before that I am an aggressive type, and on the playground of this all-white school I proceeded to take over in typical Rose Butler fashion.

I'd get those little girls out on the schoolyard at recess and I'd organize them. "Now we're going to play Farmer in the Dell," I'd say. "You can be the farmer."

"Rosie, let me be the farmer!" someone would beg.

Well, I'd just boss the whole schoolyard and the kids let me. The white teachers looking out through the school windows resented a little colored girl taking over the schoolyard and operating it during the free period. After several staff conferences, one of the teachers went to see my mother. The teacher was so polite about the trouble that Mother never did discover what was really wrong, but I knew.

The teacher told Mother that I ought to be trained to speak, that I could recite so nicely and that the faculty knew someone who could train me in speaking during recess period. Furthermore, the teacher confided, it wouldn't cost a cent.

Mother's reaction was typical, for she didn't have any pride in me at the time. "Rosie talks too much now," she told my teacher. "She doesn't need to be trained to talk. She needs to be trained to work!"

So the teachers started taking turns coming out on the schoolyard during recess periods, and they took over the organization of the games we played.

At this point the family attended Morgan Memorial Church. It was a church of all people, not a Negro church, a wonderful church, and it was the home church of the Goodwill Industries. Here I met Miss Jane Dann of Indianapolis, who had come to Boston to work in some of the insurance company offices. Miss Dann and a number of other young persons volunteered their services for the numerous programs at Morgan Memorial Church.

The church operated a Saturday school which taught young people crafts and practical skills. The boys learned industrial crafts, and the girls went to sewing and cooking classes on alternate Saturdays. In sewing class I made a tea towel, a pillowcase, a shoe bag and a stocking bag, important items in those days. In cooking class you started with oatmeal and worked up to a Christmas plum pudding. The penny you paid didn't cover the cost of even the ma-

73

terials you used, but it let you know that everything has a price.

There was also under the sponsorship of Morgan Memorial Church a wonderful summer-camp program and a tremendous Sunday school. And Miss Dann was a wonderfully young, vivacious, fascinating, interested teacher who taught me both on Saturdays and Sundays.

One day in Sunday school, during the month of October, she said anyone committing to memory the Christmas Story, the first ten verses of the second chapter of Luke, would receive a prize. Apparently she meant for us to commit these verses to memory by Christmas. I went home and memorized the Second Chapter of the Gospel of Luke and then next Sunday recited the entire chapter without assistance.

Miss Dann was impressed. She visited our house and talked to my mother, but again Mother did not have any pride in what my teacher was saying.

"Yes, she's lazy," my mother said. "All she wants to do is read. She will hide the pots and pans in the oven to keep from washing them. She just wants to read. I'm afraid she is growing up to be slovenly."

In our house slovenly was pronounced "sloben'ly" and had all the connotation of a dirty word, like today calling someone a Communist. I was horrified, and Miss Dann didn't know what to say. She simply told Mother that a girl so quick to learn should be encouraged in her studies.

Following this visit by another of my teachers, Mother commenced to pay more attention to me. Also, I didn't want to be slovenly, so I began trying to be more helpful. I learned that if I did some of the things Mother thought important, it was possible to arrange for me to do some of the things I thought were important.

For example, Mother would set me to washing the diapers, for there was always a baby at our house. In those days you had the stationary tub with two faucets, for hot and cold water, each with a round wheellike handle. This proved ideal, for I could prop my open book behind the two faucet handles and read and work on the diapers at the same time. The only problem was that I paid more attention to the book than to the diapers and often scrubbed holes in them before realizing it. Mother would take the book off the faucet and whack me on the head with it as she held up the torn remains of the diaper.

"You're coming to some bad end," Mother would say. "Rosie, I just don't know where you came from."

Mother had no understanding of fiction. The extent of her reading was the Housekeepers Column in the Boston *Daily Globe*. Fiction was, in her thinking, a complete waste of time.

However, I finally came to my senses and realized that I had to meet Mother halfway. That's how I became such a good shirt ironer and learned to do other chores rapidly, so Mother would let me sit down with my book.

Of course, we didn't have books ourselves. We couldn't afford them. This led to my acquaintance with a wonderful institution, the neighborhood public library.

This was an age populated by the Gentle Americans. Instead of feeling the necessity to have two cars in each garage, they felt it socially proper to have a library in their homes. Many an emerging middle-class American, not really understanding what Dr. Charles Eliot of Harvard meant when he said that all the books a cultured man needed to know would fit on a five-foot bookshelf, started buying volumes of classic literature which measured precisely five feet. Both the immigrant from Europe and the immigrant from south of the Mason-Dixon line put great store in education. They bought five-foot bookshelves and filled them with books, although they had not the education to comprehend all this knowledge from Plato to Dickens. Books were easy to buy on the installment plan, and, in the eyes of the emerging middle class at least, their possession alone made one look erudite. In that day there was great emphasis on books.

Our branch library, called the South End Branch of the Boston Public Library, stood just around the corner from our house on West Canton Street. In my recollection the library was housed in what might have been a former church building. This part of Boston was then inhabited largely by recently arrived foreigners, principally Italians and Portuguese, and some immigrant Negroes. Undoubtedly the branch library had been placed there in an effort to bring to the blighted area more of the cultural opportunites for which Boston was noted.

I loved to enter the library through the front entrance, climb the wide steps and push open the swinging double doors leading into a slate-floor vestibule. Beyond the vestibule extended a hallway, on either side of which were the reading rooms. I would always peer inside each reading room.

In the wintertime the cannel coal would be blazing in the fireplace grates, but in the summer the rooms were tall and wonderfully cool. They contained a distinctive smell, the blending of clean old wood and musty old books with the dry dustiness of the city's dirt.

The room also contained long reading tables over which hung green glass-shaded gas jet lamps which cast flickering circles of yellowish light. In the background stood the shelves of books, more books than I had thought existed in the entire world.

One room in particular intrigued me. The bookshelves were plainly labeled: Poet's Corner, Novelist's Corner, Explorer's Corner. I always measured my height against the door jamb of this room and wondered how much longer I had to wait before admittance to that innermost sanctum.

Actually, it was several years before my reading skills and language comprehension permitted me to make the transfer to the big reading rooms upstairs. My father had to come to the library to vouch for my character and responsibility and to prove himself a citizen in good standing. Then I had that wonderful adult library card. All the knowledge of the world, or so it seemed to me, was now as close to me as the library shelves. I was thrilled. The first adult book I checked out was Owen Wister's *The Virginian*. Also, there had miraculously sprung up on all the shelves, like the first crocus of spring, the novels of Henry James. I devoured them.

Looking back, I know that a fine collection of books can get into one's nervous system and last a lifetime. That New England autocrat Dr. Oliver Wendell Holmes said, "Above all things, as a child, a man should have tumbled about a library. All men are afraid of books who have not handled them from infancy."

Today I often wonder about my poor children who have no more "book learning" at home than I did, but also have no neighborhood library program. How do they climb aboard these vanishing years of the twentieth century when they can't read?

The downstairs part of the building had been given over to the Children's Library. At the end of the upstairs hallway you started down a narrow stairway which led through another set of swinging doors. Now you were in the children's reading room. The room was large and airy and well ventilated and filled with a number of small round tables and chairs of suitable height for children.

The room was presided over by a charming woman who greeted us by name after a few visits. The librarian always dressed in a crisp gingham dress, with freshly starched white collar and cuffs, and incredibly white rubber-soled shoes. She had a sweet smile, classical features, and her New England speech remained at all times calm, flat, and clear. She had a large number of workers who came in, I suspect, from Simmons College and the other colleges in the Boston area that offered Library Science.

The books, ever so many of them, stood lined up on open racks, and we could take them down and look at them. As I recall, they were not much like the children's books of today.

One whole section was devoted to fairy tales. There were the red fairy tales, the green fairy tales, and the yellow fairy tales, all telling about the good fairies, the dreadful ogres, the terrible giants, and the many things which filled the imaginative life of a child. We have learned since then how these fairy tales sometimes upset a child's personality by causing him to live too much in a world of make-believe. However, we enjoyed these stories very much because no matter how many heads got chopped off, they would all be put back again before the story ended. The wicked people were always punished and the good people always rewarded.

Today, if you want your child to know the story of Little Red Riding Hood, you should read the story to the child before he starts the first grade. Children today start scoffing at make believe so early in life that they themselves discredit fairy tales. So it is off to the full plot and fierce "character" roles depicted on TV, after which the children go around looking for situations that have increasing conflict. Not finding such events in most communities, the children pull wings off flies, step on June bugs, etc.

If I had a child of preschool age today, I would read him some fairy tales. It was important in my childhood, and is now, to have a child dream dreams. Of course, the child should not become just a dreamer; but often such dreams bring out the best in a person and make them creative. We need creativity today.

Another section of those bookshelves contained the series books—the great American dream which told you that however poor you were, if you did right you'd come into your own. It never was true. If you wanted to get rich, you took a gang of poor boys and worked them hard and took the lion's share of the income. But has arguing over wages and hours worked any better than scheming about profits?

Let the truth come out; those series stories were good, very good: *Five Little Peppers, Bobbsey Twins, Rover Boys, Horatio Alger,* the *Little Colonel,* and the *Elsie Dinsmore* books. I read them all.

Take the *Little Colonel.* The series started when she was a child and followed up her adventures until she had matured into a young lady. Nor did the stories duck issues. In fact, most of those series were better than people knew. In the *Little Colonel* series, when the heroine had reached the age of puberty she was at a school orchestra practice. A violin string broke and at this sudden sound the Little Colonel broke into unreasonable tears, then a very typical adolescent girl's reaction. (Mother and I had quite a discussion after I read that book.)

And how different this reaction, this behavior of a beloved friend, compared to the behavior of the once-met neurotic lad encountered in *The Catcher in the Rye,* which I know is required reading today in many high school classes.

Our library had entire shelves filled with books of poetry. I loved to commit poems to memory because I enjoyed the sound as well as the meaning of the words. Today, when it isn't winter, I will find myself trying to check my retention on parts of John Greenleaf Whittier's inspiring "Snowbound":

> The sun that brief December day
> Rose cheerless over fields of gray
> And, darkly circled, gave at noon
> A sadder light than waning moon.

Such poems permitted moments to be shared with my friends, but most of all, with my family. We were encouraged to recite at the dinner table, or around the stove at night, and I have never been bashful.

I discovered that Mother's Housekeeper's Column in the newspaper told about books for children, and knowing that Mother always read the column, I read it too. That is how I got my first book. The columnist told the mothers that they should buy or read to their children a new Robert Louis Stevenson book called *A Child's Garden of Verses.* I begged Mother to buy me that book. I begged and begged until I got it. I read every poem in that book. Most were not long, but they were very worthwhile poems, and I prized that book so much that it hardly ever was out of my sight.

This was the only time I can recall that begging made a

dent in our family way of doing things. Let one of us plead, "But everyone else is getting so and so"; or "Mother, why? Just tell me why?" and the answer was always the same swift, decisive, final reply.

"This is the Butler family. In the Butler family we work for the family, not for the individual. Your request doesn't measure up to the family needs, wouldn't you agree? We do things the Butler way!"

Mother's newspaper column also informed me of which books I should be requesting the librarian to reserve for me.

The librarian permitted each child to take out two books at a time. I would return the next day for new books. The librarian was startled that I read so fast. I read while washing, I read while bathing, I read after the family went to bed.

The librarian always asked me about the content of the books I had read. Yes, even in Boston I found companionship in those books, and received reward in a librarian's interest and encouragement.

The climax of our week always came on Wednesday nights. All we Butler children would go to the library that evening. In the springtime it would still be daylight, but in the wintertime it would already be dark. We would march into that upstairs vestibule laughing and shouting and making noise. The policeman on the beat, who had been drinking coffee in one of the office rooms, would come out. We'd suddenly turn quiet. On tiptoe, beneath his watchful eye, we would silently walk through the hallway down the stairs to the Children's Library. All the tables would be pushed back and the chairs would be arranged in a semicircle, and the storyman, as we called him, would stand up and greet us.

Ah, he was wonderful, our storyman!

For example, he would tell us the stories of Uncle Remus. As he told one of the stories, he became Uncle Remus. His eyes would be dilated and his hands would be moving and the tone of his voice would change. Of course he became part of every story he told us about. Sometimes he would stand, and then again he might sit on one of the tables.

That great roomful of children would be perfectly quiet, looking at him, sometimes laughing with him—children of all nationalities and races pushing and nudging one another in uncontrolled glee. If overly crowded we would push two chairs together and three of us would share two chairs.

I shall never forget how our storyman told us the wonderful tales of Tennyson's *Idylls of the King*. Such heroes as I had now! Sir Lancelot, Sir Galahad, and that mystic sword Excalibur. When the body of lovely Elaine came floating down on the flower-strewn barge, the storyman bent nearly to the ground and spoke in a bare whisper. I'm surprised anyone could hear him over the splash of my tears.

Remember the story? Honor—honor was something. We knew what honor meant. Tennyson had told us. Today we often do not face up to the consequences of our own acts.

At the close we would all rush to the storyman and talk at once. Everyone had the same question.

"What are you going to tell us next week? What are you going to tell?"

He'd say, "Well, I don't know yet, but when next week comes you'll know. Maybe we'll have *The Perils of Pauline*."

We would all laugh at his joke. We knew he was too good for *The Perils of Pauline*.

"I'll have something for you next week, boys and girls," he would say. "Good night!"

We would share a few more words with him and then go home, talking all the way about the wonderful people in the story. As I said, we did not live far from the library, so we were the first to part from our friends. After an evening with the storyman, I usually wanted to lie down in the dark and see the stories all over again in the mirror of my mind.

I know we were better people because of these vivid story experiences, and because of the spiritual sharing that the closeness of our friends and neighbors generated.

Once in a while either the librarian or the storyman would take us to the main library, not far away. This big white marble structure overlooked Copley Square. Inside, its beauty became almost overpowering. For me it had a special fascination, for painted on the walls below the ceiling, in reds, crimsons, and golds, were the most beautiful murals depicting scenes from the *Idylls of the King*. I could sit in the main library and look at the pictures by the hour.

Now in the fourth grade at the Everett School, I had an extremely rich literary experience. The established custom of the Boston city schools of that day dictated that each class select a class poet. In the fourth grade we selected Longfellow for our poet. The teacher suggested each student have a poet's corner at home and read some of Longfellow's poetry each day.

I told my mother, and she scraped together seventy-nine cents to buy me a volume of Longfellow's complete poems. When I think of the sacrifice it was for her to put nickels and dimes and pennies into the sugar bowl to accumulate seventy-nine cents, I shudder. But what joy it was to read and memorize Longfellow's poems that year in the fourth grade. . . .

I marvel at this intensive study of one poet, in which we probed the depth of his thought and method of expression. It was a better way of teaching than we have now. Today we try to fit words and meanings to the concepts of what the child can understand and knows about, rather than stretching his line of reasoning. Let me cite an example of how our minds were stretched. Our teacher had us cut pictures out of magazines and then match these to lines of poetry. I had found a picture of mighty rapids, and vainly tried to match it to the quiet words of Longfellow's description of the River Charles:

River that in silence windeth . . .

The teacher called me to her desk and said she did not think the picture quite fitted the poem, which we now read together. I could clearly see that my teacher was right, and mentally I grew a cubit or whatever the measurement of one's growth is under such circumstances.

That same year, however, I earned the distinction of being "industrially poor." My industrial-arts class met in the afternoon, and one day my teacher sent me home for not agreeing with her. I hadn't really disagreed with her. I had just said that "any fair-minded person would agree with me."

This school had scheduled three housekeeping classes, with my class in the afternoon being the last such class of the day. This particular day our assignment was to learn how to mop a floor. In my case this was superfluous instruction, but that didn't irritate me.

In those days the instructors were "it." No one questioned their judgment, so I was wrong; but knew I was right.

The industrial-arts instructor did not change her instructions from one class to the next. Therefore before our class met, two classes had already mopped, sponged, and dried the same floor area that day. To make matters worse, only one corner of the industrial-arts classroom had been cleaned. The instructor told us to mop the same area of floor again. Obviously, it was the same bit of floor, because one could still see the water in the cracks between the boards.

I simply told her I would not mop that particular piece of floor.

She wanted to know why.

I told her. Then I said I would mop any other part of the room she wanted mopped, because the rest of the floor needed mopping and had not been mopped that day. However, she would not agree to this.

I told her, "This is just busy work, a waste of time! Any fair-minded person would agree with me!"

She sent me home.

Instead of going home I went to a nickelodeon, saw the matinee show, and then went home. However, my girl friend, thinking I had gone right home, came bursting right in on my family, so eager to learn what had happened to me for being sent home from school.

Next day my father called on the industrial-arts teacher. That night Father confirmed my mother's worst fears. "The teacher just said that Rosie is industrially poor," Father said.

"I knew it! I knew it!" my mother said. "Industrially poor! She should be learning to do things instead of reading all the time."

It was decided that I should get a Saturday job, which for

a Boston Negro girl of those days meant housecleaning and scrubbing. So in the fourth grade I went to work. I didn't really mind, for I turned my earnings over to Mother, and I knew my contribution would help our family.

I don't recall what my Aunt Lill brought me then, but it was something that perked up my spirits. Aunt Lill stood five foot two and wore a size-nine dress, had married well and had more than the ordinary economic security, but no children. As a result, Aunt Lill was the one who brought luxury into our lives. She would come loaded with roller skates, raincoats, or the latest-style galoshes. She purchased the sort of things we would not have had but for her love of my mother and her endurance of us.

The Butler children were not always the most courteous to Aunt Lill. We felt she was much too bossy and meddlesome, always telling our mother, "I wouldn't let those children do that, Frances."

Aunt Lill meant well. The price you paid for her love was a kind of continuous and overt nagging.

She and my grandfather William encouraged my mother to let us go to the summer camp of Morgan Memorial Church, called Winning Farm. The camp offered a program of religion, arts, crafts, and athletics. My sister Mary and I went summer after summer, and we benefited greatly from the training in teamwork. Different groups did the dishes every day, and if you washed you didn't have to dry and clean up; or you set the table or cleaned your room, and some evenings you led in the devotions. You also had a chance to ask the blessing at the table. It was training as well as fun. There was absolutely no cost, not even for transportation. The only expense was for your camp clothes and their upkeep, a sort of uniform so that nobody would have better things than the rest.

It was during my year in the fifth grade, the year we studied John Greenleaf Whittier as our class poet, that the Butler family moved from Boston to Newport, Rhode Island.

Chapter 4

NEWPORT

My father had a sister, quite secure financially, who lived in Newport. After a visit there, Father felt that in this smaller place the children would be better off than in a big city like Boston. His sister, our Aunt Amanda, for whom I was given my middle name, encouraged the idea and looked forward to enjoying "the children." My mother made a trip to Newport with the two youngest children. As a result of this conference, we moved to Rhode Island.

In many ways Newport was different from Boston. There was no concentration of the poor in any special section of the city. The foreigners were for the most part Portuguese from the Cape Verde Islands. The schools were traditional but thorough. Actually, we received a better education in Newport than we would have gotten in Boston.

For years Mother worked as a clean-up woman for the

New England Steamship Company, cleaning staterooms on the old Fall River Line of boats to New York, until the strong lye became too much for her hands. Then she worked for a private old ladies' home on Narragansett Bay. By this time my two brothers, my sister Mary, and I had jobs. In our family, when you came of age you moved up and did your bit for the family. No one dissented. We didn't know we could.

My mother continued to read the Housekeeper's Column in the Boston *Daily Globe*. At that time one of the column's most prolific letter writers, a provocative and yet sensible thinker, signed herself "June Girl." The Butler family was constantly given the explanation, "This is just the way June Girl says it should be done."

Our father was a capable brickmason, and work was plentiful in Newport. His sister made the initial contact, but Father's skill secured his job. As a result, whenever possible, our father dressed to the hilt and toured the neighborhood bragging about the accomplishments of his family.

Although Aunt Lill and Grandpa William frequently came for visits, and our High Priestess came once on an excursion, Mother felt the separation from her family. Being the oldest girl in our home, Mother's loneliness drew me closer to her. She shared with me her thoughts and her hopes for her children. Also, I was bigger and stronger than she, and since our sister Charlotte was born about this time, there was a lot for me to do around the house.

We were quick to adapt to our new environment. At the fishing docks in Newport, certain fish were given away for the asking. Usually these were the large soft fish like hake and pollack, and fish that had been bitten, which often occurred when mackerel fought in the nets. So, when the fishing boats reached the docks, we would be there to collect our share of the catch, and proudly haul it home, where we would bone and salt and store the fish for use in the winter.

Soon after we came to Newport, I began working. My first job was at a boarding house for $1.50 a week. I kept fifty cents as my allowance for my personal use and Sunday school money, and gave Mother a dollar for her household expenses. The wages were not much, but I acquired valuable working experience which made my job references more impressive. My mother, however, was not satisfied with my job. She did not want me to work in any place where she felt I would not learn anything. With so many fashionable homes in Newport, I soon learned all about oyster forks, Wedgwood china, Fostoria glasses, sterling silver, and cut-glass bowls. By the time I reached college age, my earnings were $15.00 a week. I still retained fifty cents for myself and gave my mother a dollar; I saved $13.50 each week for my college expenses.

We had been in Newport only a few years when my grandfather William died. All of the Butlers went to Boston for the funeral, but even beloved Malden did not now seem the same. The big rambling house echoed our desolation.

Our High Priestess should have moved in with my greatuncle John, the well-heeled carriage-trade member of the family. Uncle John, one of Ann Elizabeth's two sons left in Virginia when she came to Boston, had later joined her in New England. He was a well-paid servant and the leading bass soloist at the Twelfth Baptist Church. He was always aware of his affluence, and now fully expected his mother to move in with his family.

Charlotte Ann Elizabeth knew that at Uncle John's house

the ladies never came downstairs unless they were dressed, for they had to act out their roles as rich people. Grandma knew she couldn't come down to the kitchen in her wrapper and slippers, or forget to put in her false teeth, or exercise a few other freedoms she enjoyed. Thus she announced her decision to live with "Frances and the children."

We were very happy about this, and shortly our High Priestess moved to Newport to be with us, and at once became monarch of all she surveyed.

At Newport I attended the Calvert School, and in the sixth grade ran for the position of Secretary of the Civic League, a big affair at that school. Literally, I had the job in my pocket. The pupils all wanted me, and nobody else elected to contest my nomination. To me this appeared perfectly natural, as though everything were waiting for me which I sincerely believed to be the truth. My grandma said this was so and I believed her. An awareness that I might not make it to the top of that league simply had never occurred to me.

At a student assembly the principal of Calvert School told the student body that she had withdrawn my name from the election because she felt this position belonged to a student in a higher grade since there was a large amount of outside correspondence to be handled, and on and on she went.

Fortunately she did talk and talk, for her words gradually alerted me that this was not so much a question of race prejudice as a snobbish feeling that poor people should be kept in their proper social relationship. I did not have the economic and social status this woman sought in the student-elected Secretary of the Civic League. Of course, I did not understand all of this at that time, but I did know the situation represented a new problem, something different in my life, which I would have to learn how to manage.

Love My Children

In the seventh grade I attended the Cranston School. There was a bad situation here. The teacher was an elderly gentleman with a whiskered face. His name was Chase, and he should have been retired. His pupils acted as bad as homemade sin, and used to sing this little ditty right to his face:

> Farmer Chase ran a race
> up and down the pillowcase.
> He fell into the fireplace
> and burned the whiskers off his face.

I mention this only to point out that when a student's eagerness to learn is thwarted, especially by a poor teacher, the natural reaction is to strike back in resentment and frustration. We all do some very mean things under the stimulus of our disappointments and succumb to the so human reaction of getting even.

In the eighth grade I attended the Clark School in the old Townsend Industrial Building. Then, in much of New England, you started in kindergarten and went through nine grades of elementary schooling. I took my ninth grade at the Munford School and had just a wonderful time. Here we had departmental teaching and some really expert teachers.

My science and mathematics teacher was Miss Hammett. She had no concern for modern methods, was totally undiplomatic, and was a tremendous teacher.

Even now I would call her the typical stereotype of the "schoolmarm" of that era. She wore a large full skirt gathered at the waist. The skirt had a huge pocket in the side seam out of which hung a tape on which she carried her keys. She wore a shirtwaist with collar and sometimes had a little bow at the neck. Her hair was parted in the middle and swept back. It softened a little on each side and then was wound up in a tight ball pulled up at the nape of the neck. Her feet were always covered with common-sense cantilever shoes.

Miss Hammett firmly believed that everybody in her room ought to learn everything that she taught. Since she taught algebra, everybody who entered her class was expected to know algebra when she had finished. However, she thought it took each person the same length of time to master a problem.

One day, for example, she taught and drilled us how to factor Case II.

To the class she said, "Now say behind me, 'A plus B squared is equal to A squared plus 2 AB plus B squared.'"

We repeated it with her.

"Now, say it again: 'A plus B squared is equal to A squared plus 2 AB plus B squared.'"

I then had the problem clearly in mind and stopped repeating it.

Miss Hammett interrupted the class and pointed her finger at me.

"Rose Butler, do you expect me to teach you algebra?"

I wanted to say I didn't care, but knew better. Such impertinence wasn't polite. My mother and father would have been disgraced.

I said, "Yes."

"All right, begin again," Miss Hammett said.

She made me say, "A plus B squared is equal to A squared plus 2 AB plus B squared" again and again until she and I were both tired, but I said it.

That was her method of teaching, and she was an excellent teacher. As a result of her patience I have always been an excellent student of mathematics. I realized the big difference between Miss Hammett and most other teachers. She cared. She paid attention to us.

In her class, as soon as you finished your assignment for that day, you went up to her desk. At the corner of her desk she kept a notebook with pages of problems for you to do. We tried to do these pages and get them right the first time. For one thing, there was never an end to the sets of problems. Also, as soon as you did one set of problems, your name would be placed on the board and she would state the number of problems you had done. The board might indicate you had done 125 problems, while other children hadn't finished the first problem yet. In this way she gave us a competitive spirit. Almost by brute force she made us take pride in what we were doing.

I loved my social studies teacher, Mrs. Bosworth, and she returned my affection in a most genuine manner. I eagerly tried to do everything she wanted done plus a little bit more. (When studying the circulatory system of the body for my science class, I made my sister Mary lie down on a piece of wrapping paper. I outlined Mary's body, and then filled in with red and blue pencils all the arteries and veins.)

Mrs. Bosworth was the first person who ever spoke to me about going to college. I had never given college a thought. She started me thinking about teaching, and her personal interest thrilled me.

However, Mrs. Bosworth did more than just talk about college. She knew a West Indian doctor, a Dr. Marcus Wadsworth, who was a trustee of Howard University in Washington, D. C.

This concerned teacher had Dr. Wadsworth call on my

94

parents and talk to them about my attending Howard
University after finishing my high school training. Now I
don't believe my parents had ever heard of Howard University, but somehow they learned that Dr. Wadsworth had
sent his daughter to Wellesley. By some intuitive sixth sense
they decided that this well-intentioned man wanted something less for me than he had provided for his own daughter.
That they had absolutely no money and no knowledge of
what either school cost (or that Wellesley had but a few
Negro students at that time) was quite immaterial to my parents. There could be but one answer to Dr. Wadsworth.
No!

Of course, it is interesting to note that Mrs. Bosworth,
who gave me straight A's and evidenced sincere interest in
my welfare and wanted me to earn my college degree, apparently never considered the possibility of my attending a
state university closer to home.

For some years I never entertained such an idea either.

The joy of my life was Rogers High School, an intellectual
school devoted to preparing people for college. Of course, even
Rogers was not perfect, for it did have a caste system. Outside of the academic contacts, the Jewish and Negro pupils
had little or no social contact with other students. This
was by design. For instance, dancing was permitted during
lunch period. It would not have appeared right for people
of certain status to dance with persons from a different status
level. Schedules were therefore carefully arranged so that
your lunchtime came at the proper period for you to inter-
mingle with your own social-status group.

During my first year at Rogers High School, I took
courses in English, English History, Latin, and Algebra. The

second year my English class devoted several months to a thorough study of my old friend, *The Idylls of the King,* and I experienced the joys of a literary homecoming.

At this point I decided to take a commercial course on the side. I wanted to master typing and to learn proper business-letter forms, achievements which I might need in college. At Rogers everyone talked about college, and I had just started to think seriously about preparing myself for such an eventuality.

When I signed up for the typing class, I received a jolt. The typing teacher would not accept me. She didn't want me in her class. This teacher was a very sincere person and took a great deal of pride in the fact that she could place in a suitable business office all graduates of her classes. She instinctively recognized the fact that she would never be able to place me in any such position. Therefore, she did not want the responsibility of training me for something which she knew I could not hope to achieve.

I had talked with this teacher but a few minutes before realizing something was wrong. Fortunately I put my finger on it when I said, "Well, I don't want a job. I am going to college!"

The teacher smiled one of those deprecating smiles that the person of superior intelligence reserves for the inexperienced, but she said nothing.

A Miss Ruth Franklin, the guidance counselor, who had taken an interest in me, spoke up. "Rose is smart. She will learn; you take her!"

I was admitted to the commercial course.

Also at this school we had a music teacher whose teaching abilities I have never seen equaled. Each year his classes worked on a cantata. One year the cantata was about the biblical character Ruth, and another year it was *Faust*. We studied more than the parts. We studied the music and the history of the opera and the composer. I worked on the "Soldiers' Chorus," and I remember to this day our little group singing :

Now home again we come, the long and fiery strife of battle over.
Rest in pleasant after toil as hard as ours beneath a stranger sun.

We sang our part over and over again in pursuit of excellence.

"Remember, you're telling it to somebody," our teacher reminded us. "You want everybody to hear your words. You want your tones to be nice and round."

We articulated.

We put forth every effort to develop the finished product for the sake of the finished product and the standards we represented. The purpose was not to make money or show off, for we never produced either cantata. We were not permitted to prepare a show. We were taught to love the music and the story for what they would mean to each of us.

When I made my mark in the commercial class, Miss Ruth Franklin, the guidance counselor, renewed her personal interest in me and spoke to the principal, Mr. Thompson, who was on the Board of Regents of Rhode Island State Normal School. Mr. Thompson spoke to the Rhode Island Normal Admissions Office, and they agreed to accept me in their teacher training program if I would take more American History and some art courses.

Therefore, I took an additional half year's postgraduate

work at Rogers High School. However, just before my graduation, tragedy struck. Charlotte Ann Elizabeth Lindsey, our High Priestess, died. This was 1916, and Grandma had reached the remarkable age of 107 years.

Charlotte Ann Elizabeth had been in failing health for some time, but because of her age nobody had been greatly alarmed. She had been to a doctor, who insisted on placing her on a strict diet. Our High Priestess did not have a good opinion of that doctor or his special diet. She would let us children know when she wanted to eat something off her diet, and we'd get it for her.

If Mother discovered this deception, she would scold us as well as Grandma.

"I ate it because I wanted it," our High Priestess would say. "Frances, the Lord will call me when he wants me, and no fool doctor's going to change that."

Finally it became apparent to all of us that Grandma was failing. The doctor had her placed in a hospital. Uncle John came down from Boston and he was furious. He was sorry there was no one in this whole house to take care of his loved one. Now strangers had to care for his mother.

He ignored the fact that the High Priestess had chosen to live with us, instead of with him. And all the time the High Priestess had been living with us Uncle John had contributed nothing toward her support—nor had he ever been asked to do so.

Some of us told him off, which didn't help smooth over the situation, for tempers were on edge.

Then Charlotte Ann Elizabeth Lindsey died.

My Uncle John did an unpardonable thing. He had her body taken from the hospital to Boston and buried from the Twelfth Baptist Church. He did this without even con-

sulting my mother. The High Priestess had been in Newport with us for six years, and for a like number of years
before moving from Malden had been unable to maintain
regular church attendance. There was literally no one left
at the Twelfth Baptist Church who remembered this once
vigorous and faithful communicant. But Uncle John had
his way.

Tempers were so short that only Mother and my eldest
brother John went to Boston for the funeral. The rest of the
Butler family stayed home.

Personally, I cried and didn't eat for three days.

I lay on my bed most of the time, my white graduation
dress spread beside me. Our High Priestess had thought my
graduation dress very lovely. Aunt Lill had helped pay for
the dress, but now my life's most exciting moment paled into
despair. My High Priestess would not be at Rogers High
School to see me graduate. She had been both at John's and
Bob's graduation. She had insisted that their high school
diplomas be framed and hung in prominent positions in our
living room, uncontestable proof of our family's education.

In those lonely days, with the High Priestess gone to her
eternal home at last, and Mother gone to Boston for the funeral, I began to realize just how much drive and push this
dear woman had given to our family. I vowed never to disgrace the family tree which she had planted on New England's free soil by sheer determination and her will to find
freedom.

Strange, too, but I believe this was the first time I ever
understood my great-grandfather, Reuben Lindsey. I knew
now how he must have felt, loving her, and she loving him
and yet having to leave him.

Reuben Lindsey had died some years before. He had

left some property in a section of Norfolk called Ghent. The land was sold and his estate divided among myriad relatives, each of whom received the magnificent sum of $140. This was just like money from home. Everyone was delighted, and poor Reuben Lindsey at last came into his own.

Also, I realized how deeply rooted our lives were in the traditional values our High Priestess had given us. Grandma could not read, although she knew long passages from the Holy Bible. She always carried her Bible with her, and frequently led us in family Bible reading. She never preached to us or at us, but taught us spiritual values by precept and example. She gave us a system of values tied to the Lord and these we live by today.

She helped us to make a great event out of each birthday, and in our family we had a good many birthdays. They all fell between January and July, including our parents' birthdays, and I believe our High Priestess looked forward to each celebration with as much anticipation as the person who had the birthday. In our family you chose the dinner menu on your birthday, knowing that Mother would rob her sugar bowl to get what you wanted. Dessert for birthday dinners never changed. It was ice cream made in the home freezer. On your birthday you got to lick the dasher when it was removed from the churn. Mother always left enough on for the birthday child to enjoy.

On your birthday Father said grace at the table, and the Lord was always thanked for sending the Butlers such a fine child. You sat in a place of honor. You got a present. It was just a simple family affair, but it was part of our family's system of values which we still carry on today.

Christmas was another gala time. When I was very small,

we journeyed to Malden for Christmas, but after Grandmother Rose died, Grandfather William and Charlotte Ann Elizabeth came to our house for Christmas dinner.

Oh, I was completely innocent about Christmas. When eight years old, I was still going around putting out the fires in the fireplaces so Santa Claus could come in.

Long before Christmas we would start saving our money, so we could go downtown to do our shopping. I'd probably save a whole quarter, and wind up with presents for everyone. Once you got home with your purchases, you carefully wrapped them in white tissue paper. In those days we had no boxes, so the paper had to camouflage the gift.

On Christmas morning Mother arose early, as she did every morning, and said her prayers and read some verses from the Bible. She always closed her prayer with a promise to be good and decent. We always heard her praying, and instinctively in our own manner would say our prayers too.

Then Mother would prepare a big breakfast for us and afterward dress us for church. (When in our teens we were permitted to go caroling with the church groups on Christmas Eve.)

At church there would be a beautiful Christmas tree, and eventually—after many hymns and prayers and Scripture readings, there would be a gift for each child.

Then home again, where we would give and open our family presents, and anxiously await the arrival of the High Priestess and Aunt Lill and Grandfather William, who always brought presents for each of us.

Now Christmas dinners at the Butlers' was something else. It was a big dinner with all the trimmings, from candy and nuts to cranberries. I still don't know how Mother managed, but Aunt Lill always helped, and following the recipes in the Housekeeper's Column, we put on a big one.

We would eat until we were ready to pop and were hardly able to push ourselves away from the table. Then we'd join other children for skating and sledding at the playground, only to come home cold and hungry again. Mother always had plenty of Christmas dinner leftovers for a second meal, and we would invite our friends in to share our affluence. What more proof was needed to show that we were blessed by the Lord? God was love, and love was God. Our High Priestess told us so.

Our Christmases had always been wonderful, and I reviewed every one of them during those lonesome and teary days. Then something else my High Priestess had said came to mind.

"We are children of God and must have respect for one another. Remember God is in this house and we must show him respect."

I often have thought of that statement when I visit some of our present-day homes. I am reminded of the time Jesus, as a boy, stayed behind in Jerusalem, and a frightened and half-angry Mary later found him at the temple. Jesus spoke to his mother with such humility and respect that Mary understood, even though she failed to understand the mystery of God the Father of which Jesus told her. She simply knew by his attitude that her relationship with Jesus was right.

Today we adults are so busy we don't notice that we don't give enough of ourselves to our children to establish such respect and love in their lives. When our children get noisy underfoot, we reach in our pockets and give them the $1.50

change we happen to have, and suggest they take the money and go somewhere to spend it—but go!

I know today, as I did then, that the High Priestess was right. "We are children of God and must have respect for each other."

After graduation from Rogers High School I framed my diploma and hung it prominently in our living room, just as the High Priestess would have wanted. Then I was swept up in a brand-new experience, going away to college. Oh, how the High Priestess would have been pleased.

Rhode Island Normal School is located in Providence, Rhode Island. My generous Aunt Lill put up the money for the first semester's room and board to enable me to get my feet firmly planted scholastically.

While I attended Rogers High School, my brother John had worked for the New England Steamship Company at a weekly salary of $9. From this pay he gave Mother $5 a week for room and board, laundry, and insurance. He also had given me an allowance of 25 cents a week. With the remainder of his salary he paid for his own night-school courses and bought clothes and incidentals. When I went to college my father (who never sent me a dime) decided that each of my brothers, John and Bob, would send me $2 a week to help defray my expenses. This they did, and I am sure without too much griping. As I have said, the Butlers were a close-knit family. We shared.

I thoroughly enjoyed my three years at Rhode Island Normal School, although between a heavy scholastic load and a full work load (I did receive a work scholarship), I had little time for anything else. However, two rather significant events happened to me during my time at that school.

Miss Clara Craig, from whom I learned so much about Madame Montessori's teaching methods, was Director of Student Teaching and my personal friend. She was a very fine person, although her viewpoint at times was rather restricted for someone in her position.

The school was controlled by the Italian and Irish Catholics, and Miss Craig's brothers were priests. She was very devout.

One year, just before Christmas vacation, a very fine Christmas program was given by the faculty and directed by the speech teacher, a Miss Patterson. In the program was a short dramatic skit called "Solomon's Pockets." The story was about a little Negro boy who stole everything in sight and stuffed his loot into his pockets. Finally it was decided to sew up the openings of his pockets as a way to keep him from stealing.

The line that triggered my emotional system was Solomon's mother saying to him, "You're just a no-'count nigger, and nobody thinks anything of you."

During the course of the story Solomon became honest and stopped stealing, and at Christmas he was given a new suit with pockets in it.

After the program I went to the platform and Miss Patterson was smiling and I am certain expected me to offer congratulations on the program. When I failed to volunteer an opinion she asked how I had liked the program.

"With all of the American and English literature available, why did you have to present such a feature? You have at least three Negroes in this school and the word that you used is not acceptable."

She said, "Oh. Come into my office. Come into my office!"

"No," I said. . . . "It's Christmas and I'm going home."

At home I told my mother what had happened, and she completely surprised me.

"You did just right, Rose. I hope you were courteous as you talked to Miss Patterson."

I said, "Yes, Mother, I was courteous. I don't know anything else, but I did tell her how I felt."

"You did just right if you were courteous, for it was not a good story for Christmas."

This marked the first time my mother had recognized me as an adult, worthy of having opinions which contradicted those of an older person. Formerly Mother would have said, "Now Miss Patterson is older than you, and I am certain she knew better than you."

Although I had been close to my mother before, even a helpmate, this new feeling of comradeship established us as two women. For the first time in my life I could contradict a grown person and still hold my mother's esteem. From then on I became my mother's "mother," the one who advised and encouraged her.

After the Christmas holidays Miss Craig came to me. She said, "I just don't know why Miss Patterson did it. It spoiled Christmas for all of us. You didn't know, but members of the faculty were just petrified to think she would do such a thing."

Then Miss Craig let slip what had really disturbed her. "Did you know that a month ago she gave a play and had a Jewish child making the sign of the cross?"

While I was at Rhode Island Normal School, it was announced that the famous Sarah Bernhardt was making her final American tour and would give dramatic readings at Fay's Theatre. Student tickets were available.

I had read that this actress had some kind of personal magnetism which made her the toast of Europe and had won her the highest acclaim in America. One of her legs had been amputated, and it was stated that Miss Bernhardt would be seated on a pillow on stage throughout the performance. I thought the picture in the newspaper made her look like an old witch; I could just imagine her voice cracking. Most students were talking about the forthcoming Bernhardt performance, but I definitely was not taking my small allowance and parting with it for such a treat. I simply didn't know enough about the stage presence of Sarah Bernhardt.

However, Aunt Lill rushed to college and stated, "Rose, you are going! This is the chance of a lifetime. Her last tour!"

Aunt Lill gave me the money, so I got dressed and went to see Sarah Bernhardt.

I have never been anyplace where the atmosphere was so electrified. Before her appearance everyone was talking and yet you could feel the tension in the air. It just vibrated.

When the curtains parted, some men carried Miss Bernhardt out on a pillow. They placed her on the stage floor, front and center. Suddenly everyone was standing up, screaming and clapping. It was almost like our teen-agers now when their favorite singing group makes a personal appearance, although not wild to quite such an extent. There was some reverence and awe in that demonstration.

Her voice was cracked and she did look like a witch, but I can feel to this day the waves of personal magnetism by which she drew her audience close to her. I was enthralled, and next day on campus I was glad that I too could say I had seen the great Bernhardt.

My mother was so pleased to learn that I had gone to see Bernhardt that I have always suspected Mother asked my Aunt Lill to make me go. Mother wanted me to enjoy this rich cultural experience which I had been ready to pass up.

While at Rhode Island Normal School, I did my practice teaching at the Coggeshall School in Newport. This proved to be a landmark experience, confirming my desire to be a teacher.

At the Coggeshall School there had been some hesitation about accepting me, a Negro. Even when accepted, I was assigned some of the unusual problems. The fact that I overcame these problems and became a loved and respected teacher eliminated any doubts others had of my becoming a teacher.

In my classes were slow readers and children with special learning needs, and hovering nearby was the irate parent who simply knew that his or her child was not getting the needed attention. Obviously, if I was to survive at the Coggeshall School, things had to be done differently. So I did them differently. Instead of singing the scale—do, re, me, fa, sol, la, ti, do, re—we learned rhythm by stepping to the music of the waltz, and when we had mastered this we were ready to learn about the musical scale found in the waltz. By trying to show a practical motive for learning a given subject, I soon had most of the children reasonably happy and productive. Most of all, my children knew they had a teacher who loved them and wanted to help them.

However, as any teacher will tell you, winning the class helps, but it does not mean you have won the parents. Today many teachers load their classes with homework, not because they think it does the pupil any good but because they know the parents expect it. How else can parents be certain that Johnny is getting a good education?

For the first parents' night I followed already established procedures, and it was terrible. The whole class would be at the blackboard, at all levels of attainment, and the parents had absolutely no way of evaluating progress other than to note their own little cherub wasn't doing too well. "Now teacher, he doesn't seem to be doing so and so. He may need special attention—just while getting started, of course."

The whole evening was simply awful, and I promptly decided to change things.

For the next parents' night, I put the children at the blackboard at their different levels of learning. In these small groups each child would compete with his own peers. I explained to the parents what I was doing and had surprisingly few questions that night. By the following parents' night, the parents could compare their child's progress within his peer group, and this for each subject area demonstrated. Parents were quick to note areas of progress as well as areas where help was needed. In most instances, after identifying the subject area of need, parents asked what special help they could give at home. This simple device of permitting the parents to see the child in relationship to peer-group progress greatly improved parents' attitudes.

My experience at the Coggeshall School revealed an important fact about my teaching career. If I, a Negro, wanted to get ahead in my chosen profession, my credentials would have to be better than those of most white applicants. This was a fact of life, and it mattered not whether you argued the polemics of its being right or wrong. A fact is a fact, and one is a fool not to recognize the truth. Therefore, I decided to go on for my Master's Degree, and enrolled at the University of Rhode Island at Kingston, Rhode Island.

The University of Rhode Island was a small southern New England college with many formal affairs. I was grateful for my Newport in-service training, for I knew just what spoon, or fork, or serving utensil to use, and my etiquette was impeccable. However, my father, never one to miss an opportunity to create an impression, sent me a dozen long-stemmed American Beauty roses on my birthday.

My two years at University of Rhode Island were pure joy. This was primarily an engineering university. I had to either register in the College of Engineering or in the School of Home Economics. I chose engineering and fell into the hands of Dr. "Buggy" Barlow, a teacher of entomology.

I started by taking general entomology, and Dr. Barlow was very much impressed with my interest, if not in my ability to chase butterflies. I soon took economic entomology. Along with my entomology I had to take physics and chemistry. From my teachers in the engineering school I learned excellent work habits, personal standards of accuracy, and a perspective for evaluating relative values. The experience further confirmed my desire to teach.

Whenever I returned to that campus after my graduation, Dr. Barlow would refer to me as his "galla nipper girl." He was recalling an embarrassing class experience.

One day he exhibited to the class some live specimens of a huge mosquitolike creature and asked if anyone recognized the insect. I raised my hand because my High Priestess had told me all about those insects.

"That's a galla nipper!" I said.

"A what?" Dr. Barlow asked.

"A galla nipper," I insisted. "And you'd better be careful, for they'll bite you."

Dr. Barlow laughed and the class joined him.

"This is a stone fly," he said, "and it does not have biting mouth parts."

I didn't care what he said. My grandma had always made us kill galla nippers because they were big and would bite.

In the kindest manner imaginable, at a later date, Dr. Barlow brought out a microscope and one of my galla nippers and we very carefully looked at it under high-power magnification. My grandma had been wrong, but so kindly did this man correct my misinformation that nothing else about my High Priestess was tarnished. So she had made a mistake about stone flies. Everyone's entitled to a mistake in 107 years of life. (What if I had to go back to the classroom and teach chemistry and physics today? Most of what I learned fifty years ago would be wrong, outdated, or bypassed by the knowledge explosion.)

Because of the weight of my engineering subjects, I concentrated my electives in the area of English literature in pursuit of soul enrichment. Again, I fell into the hands of a most gifted teacher, the late Helen Beck. She had a unique ability to get the most out of the subject material and at the same time stimulate her classes to original thinking and work. She simply loved originality and creativity. To explore the literary minds of the ages was her mission in life.

I was graduated from the University of Rhode Island in June of 1921 with a Master of Science degree. I had had five years of college training, and had earned my advanced degree from a recognized university. The New England Federation of Women's Clubs had given me a most generous scholarship those last two years. This and a job serving table in the nearby home of a Providence banker had greatly lightened the economic pinch.

The college placement bureau went to work for me, but it was really through the effort of Dr. Barlow that I secured a position on the staff of Virginia Normal and Industrial Institute, a Negro land-grant college in Petersburg, Virginia. Furthermore, since my job did not start until September, Dr. Barlow put me on his staff at the University to mount specimens and bring his files and records up to date.

PART II

THE SOUTH

Chapter 5

VIRGINIA

In September of 1921, at the age of twenty-two, I left Newport for the state of Virginia and my first teaching position. I felt somewhat like an exile returning to his homeland. Although I had heard about the rural ghettos of the South, it was my belief that all my people really needed to improve their lot in life was education, education as I knew it. I was very young, but strong of body and eager and willing to work.

On reaching Washington, D. C., I had to transfer to the Jim Crow car. This hurt. It hurt deeper than I had expected, and I wondered what my High Priestess would have said and done.

Also, it started me pondering my father's parting remarks.

"Rose, find a task no one else wants, and do it so thoroughly that you become the unquestioned expert. You must be able to stand up to criticism, just and unjust. You don't know the South, and you are fresh and headstrong. Listen and look. Don't be a crusader. Find a point of entry where you can fight segregation. Never give up principle, but don't be too proud to act with compassion toward those who treat you unjustly."

I have never forgiven my father for his abject failure to provide for his family, or at least to have tried, for I know what his failure cost my mother. Yet, my father had his points. Today I find myself still using my father's advice, given to me so long ago, with my students.

I don't know what I had expected to find at the college in Virginia, but what I found was a half-baked form of so-called higher education. In comparison to both Rhode Island schools, miseducation would be a more appropriate term, although they were trying to do with what they had.

The campus was presided over by President John Manuel Gandy, a benevolent despot.

At the time I arrived steps were under way to upgrade the faculty and thereby qualify the school for national accreditation. The purpose was to change this typical and traditional segregated agricultural and industrial institute, offering two years of college, to a segregated four-year state college. A recent Supreme Court decision had all but made mandatory this wider avenue for higher education among state-sponsored Negro colleges.

Virginia had only one state-supported institution for Negroes, so the money and effort had to be developed at Petersburg. This school would soon become Virginia State College and in 1925 would award its first four-year college diplomas.

The accreditation program had split the faculty members. Some of the present faculty, including many of the best teachers, did not have acceptable degrees. These were the teachers who had earned teaching certificates and degrees from abolitionist-founded Southern schools. These teachers had spent their whole lives in the South, and besides teaching their courses just as the outdated textbooks presented them, they also recognized a responsibility to their students to demand discipline, to teach manners, to impart some polish and culture. They themselves were a reflection of the New England schoolmarms who had picked up their skirts and gone South during the reconstruction days following the Civil War, in the ambitious hope of training and educating the Freedmen, as the former Negro slaves had then been called.

Opposed to this faculty grouping were those Negroes (also of Southern origin) who had gone north to the "Promised Land" for their education, taken chiefly at large state universities. These faculty members had earned acceptable degrees, but it did not necessarily follow that they were all good teachers. Even in the Promised Land, opportunities had been denied them because they were Negroes. Besides, their rural Southern origins had deprived them of the social experiences necessary to acquire poise and the polished manners which command respect. Thus, their college experience had proved to be a hard and lonely struggle. They had found themselves outside the student fellowship of the big Northern universities. Most of these scholastic pilgrims had finished their education without ever learning that a cultural side to college life existed, for at no turn could they find an avenue open for their participation.

For the most part the classes they taught at Virginia State

College reflected a cold and factual presentation of subject facts. Their attitudes toward their students remained a take-it-or-leave-it, I-couldn't-care-less, lack of concern.

Now these differing faculty personalities, besides being pitted against each other on the basic question of an accreditation program, were also pitted against each other in one of President John Manuel Gandy's more benevolent activities.

At Virginia State College we had chapel every day except Saturday and Sunday, and you were expected to attend religious services at one of the Negro churches in Petersburg. The college chapel programs were considered a part of each student's training, and so attendance was compulsory. Nearly every week the president lured to chapel an outside speaker, a writer, an artist, a poet, a singer. I later learned that he often signed a personal note to bring such national stars as Marian Anderson to our chapel programs.

These outside personalities were asked to submit their program well in advance so that the appropriate department —music, art, literature—might explain the background of the program to the student body. Thus, say with Marian Anderson, the students were not only listening to a great singer but listening for certain songs in her repertoire. For days the student body had been schooled in the characteristics of her announced musical numbers as well as the distinctive features of each selected composer's works.

On these special chapel days faculty and students dressed in their Sunday best, sat stiffly in chapel, and arose and applauded as a body when the artist appeared. Everyone hoped that their question (submitted in advance) might be one of those to be discussed by the visiting dignitary as he told of the work it took to succeed in his field.

These were wonderful experiences for a student body of such limited cultural contacts, and I found myself siding more and more with those Southern-trained faculty members who regarded the acquisition of manners and culture an important part of higher education.

I did not budge on my original idea that the South needed real and honest education, but in that first year in Virginia I lost seventeen pounds as well as my confidence that formal education alone would provide the total answer for my people.

Our students came from the rural South, where the migration from the fields to the cities, which had started with the opening of factory jobs during World War I, continued. They came from the newer ghettos of those same factory towns and particularly from the urban Northern cities. A pupil brought his own concept of higher education, and some pupils had no concept at all, just a burning desire to escape from their former lives. Most believed that a college education would automatically open the closed doors to the good life. The idea that you worked to get an education in order to learn how to work was too ridiculous for even casual discussion.

Even now I laugh and cry at the remembrance of those students, and when I meet old Virginia State College faculty friends we exchange news and comments about our past students. Of some we can laugh and say:

"Remember so-and-so?"

"Sure, the next thing he learns will be the first thing he learned."

"I met so-and-so in Washington. She's still so dumb she wouldn't ring if you put bells on her."

But then we had one boy who walked all the way to Vir-

ginia from Florida. He literally walked right out of his shoes
and had only the clothes on his back and no funds—only
an unquenchable desire to improve himself. Another boy
arrived in a homburg hat, chesterfield coat, and striped
pants and spats, complete with cane and a fantastic idea
of what college was all about.

I remember overhearing one newly arrived boy say, "That
Miss Butler ain't so smart as a teacher ought to be. Has to
study her lesson each day."

These kids were clever at everything except lessons.
Cheating had been an accepted way of survival in their lives,
and even the reasons for the disciplines of college had to be
taught to them. One told me, "You're so nice it hurts me to
cheat in your class."

They knew that the social order was changing, for they
weren't about to accept what their parents had taken lying
down. The problem was, they had no knowledge of where
they were going and no background of skills to carry them
anywhere. And often there existed between them and their
parents a wall of noncommunication which so often separates generations during periods of rapidly changing social
outlook.

These new social outlooks were the natural but slow evolve-
ment of emancipation. Unable after the Civil War to recon-
cile conflicting points of view—whether to punish the South
further or to reconstruct the South—the Federal Government had finally taken the easy way out.

The Freedmen, the emancipated Negro slaves who didn't
even own the clothes on their own backs, were finally given
the 15th Amendment, the right to vote, only to have the
Southern states abrogate that right by every possible device. Gradually, under the watchful eye of the Federal Gov-

ernment and especially influenced by decisions of the Supreme Court, a segregated form of education for the Negro emerged as a scant hope of escape from this climate of deprivation.

The South had yet to emerge from its agrarian economy, and its life was still geared to the cycle of crops. Most of the South's Negro elementary schools operated for only five or six months out of the year because "the children were needed in the fields." If the school board held a meeting on a proposal for six months of schooling, Negro parents would fill the hall to protest. Everyone knew the white landlords were telling the Negro parents to protest or find another tenant farm to work. There wasn't much alternative for the Negro parents, even if they disagreed with the short-term school year, which most did not. In their eyes, what could a Negro boy or girl do with an education? "Don't need no education to work in the fields."

Also, because the South was poor and needed so much for its white schools, funds left over for the Negro schools were scant. Some Negro schools had "patent seats," two or more pupils per seat, and a few had no seats at all, just sawboard-plank benches.

Even in those instances where the Negro school operated under the directive of a friendly white superintendent, progress remained shackled to the regional viewpoint. I recall asking one such superintendent for a scale for the Negro grade school, as most of the children had never been weighed.

This superintendent replied, "Miss Butler, I wish I could, but we don't have scales in all the white schools yet."

During this time the old Southern politician's argument remained constant: "The Negro has such a small brain you can't educate him much past the fifth grade, so why appropriate any more money? Besides, wouldn't an educated nigger be dangerous?" The incongruity of such double talk seemed to bother no one.

For a long time this type of talk limited Negro education pretty much to the grade-school level. However, around the start of this century, Booker T. Washington's success with his Tuskegee Institute and his idea that everyone should be taught a marketable skill had great appeal on both sides of the color line in the South. All over the old South vocational training schools were founded for the Negro. For the most part these training schools offered the equivalent of two years of high school with courses heavily weighted toward agrarian-related vocations for boys and home-making for girls.

However, in my Virginia days following World War I, the young Negro knew that something was wrong. These training schools were not providing him with the marketable skills he needed for the factories in the industrialized urban centers of growth. But suggestions for change of this agrarian emphasis met strong resistance.

Once I participated in a rural Virginia county school-board meeting, which was considering dropping the name "Institute" for the term "Preparatory School," while retaining the two-year curriculum. One of the local rednecks jumped to his feet and shouted, "Them niggers is tryin' to do away with the Institute so's they kin get 'em a four-year high school just like us white folks." He was absolutely right. The Negro wanted real education and his attitude was stiffening.

Today many Negroes recall the sham of those vocational institutes and rebel at any idea of vocational training, despite the fact that many skilled blue-collar jobs are now better paying than many white-collar jobs. There remains the old fear that somehow they'll again be hoodwinked into accepting a type of training which the economy has already bypassed.

In those days, and especially in the rural South, most elementary grade teachers in the Negro schools were girls who had graduated from one of these two-year institutes. With a training-school diploma, representing completion of the tenth grade, it was possible in most Southern states for a Negro to receive a temporary teaching certificate. If these same girls took additional courses and training and an additional state examination to upgrade themselves, some states, such as Virginia, decreed that their salary ($25 to $30 for each of the five months taught) had to be increased, often by as much as $10 for each of the five months of the school term. Many a rural county educational superintendent let it be known that the county had no funds to pay an increase to anyone who had upgraded himself, but he would promise to see that every teacher's temporary certificate was renewed.

All of this washed over me like a strange flood of despair, and on my knees in my room I thanked my High Priestess for having fled to Boston; and then wept for these, my children, who had had no Charlotte Ann Elizabeth to show them the way.

What could be done for them?

This was the beginning of the era of testing in American schools. The Negro quickly followed his white brethren and gave college-entrance examinations. The results were what was to be expected—a wide range of scores and sharp deviations from age and grade norms. The bald truth was out: Most Negro youths seeking college admissions were functionally illiterate at graduation time if compared to national norms of achievement.

This testing showed irrefutably the inherent error which existed in segregated education. There should have been a panic button for both races to press. Instead, rhetoric, that old and established Southern device, was utilized by both races, for the leaders chose to protect themselves and therefore the status quo. Nothing of a corrective nature was undertaken.

Well, if the legislative leaders and school administrators didn't get the message, I did. I set up subfreshman English and subfreshman mathematics as required noncredit courses for those pupils whose test scores indicated they might be helped by this additional work. For all of that first year at Virginia I taught these classes each afternoon in addition to my regularly assigned college courses. In fact, nearly fifty years later most Negro colleges still face these same problems, and probably have added remedial reading to the list of make-up courses.

Of course, since 1922 to the present day, standards of Negro education at both the elementary and secondary level have greatly improved, but so have those of the nation as a whole. The Negro student of segregated education still has a long run just to catch up. Thus, remedial work at the subfreshman level is standard for entirely too large a percentage of the freshman classes of our Negro colleges today.

My willingness to work, my desire to help the whole person of the student, coupled with my fine academic background, endeared me to President Gandy. He listened to me. If critical, I stated my reasons and backed them up with a proposal. He did not accept all my suggestions, but he did accept more than I had a right to expect—the remedial classes, for example. As a result, I was not the most popular faculty member with many of my colleagues.

Also, the students in my make-up classes were convinced my purpose was to make them pronounce the English language with a Boston accent. Maybe it was, for their slow, soft, slurred Southern accent often proved incomprehensible to me. If they could not pronounce a word, how could they hope to spell it? So we spent hours learning how to articulate, which I discovered had to precede the teaching of required rules of grammar and punctuation. Later I was to realize that the initial step to all make-up courses is the development of vocabulary.

Although the tasks which faced me were seemingly insurmountable, it never occurred to me to quit. First, I had nowhere to go; second, I felt impelled to arouse the people who were inclined to protect the status quo. Often they were able teachers who could have made an impact on their world, but who had lived under the restrictive conditions of the South so long that they felt change might lead to something worse.

Once again I said a prayer of praise and respect for my High Priestess who had left her family no material wealth, just a fine standard of values and personal pride.

Really, until I got to Virginia I had never met race, and then not so much race as color. If you recall, the sort of rebuffs encountered in Boston and Newport because I was a Negro had been marked down to ignorance, not hard prejudice. I still believe that what we so commonly call prejudice is but pitiful human ignorance and a blind striving to hang on to the status quo. For instance, look what happened to the stagnant economy in Atlanta once the Negro was franchised and could find work. You cannot have half the populace on relief and expect the general economy to pick up as it does when everybody receives a paycheck.

However, when I say I met color at Virginia State College I am referring to the skin color of the Negro. At that time it was fashionable in some Negro circles to think that the one way to escape being a Negro, one answer to the problem of white oppression, was to become white. There were lotions to bleach skin, and other lotions to uncurl hair. It was also considered smart to attempt to marry a light-complexioned person so that your children would be nearer the white race in features and skin color. This attitude was not strange. Everything we saw that was moving on with success was white. It appeared that "white made right."

Now in Southern Negro colleges, even to this day, one of its best fund-raising activities is the choir. Negro college choirs travel around the world giving concerts and raising needed funds. The choirs are on the go more than the athletic teams.

The college choir was recognized at Virginia State College as a potent public-relations medium. Effort was made to select pretty, well-behaved girls who would not be problems on the trips. The music directors were well prepared. In the 1920's Miss Anna Lindsay, a Fisk University graduate and an unbending disciplinarian, sought to achieve perfection in the choir. She taught all the music classes, conducted the choir, the Treble Clef Club of women, and the male chorus. Her accompanist, Miss Johnella Frazier, a Fisk graduate who had sung in the famous Fisk Choir, was an accomplished musician.

Later the music department came under the direction of a man whose general musicianship was of the highest order. However, his flair for showmanship sometimes led to heartbreak for some girls. This man desired a sound, well-balanced musical aggregation that made a good appearance. Yet, when two girls of equal talent tried out for the choir, the better-looking girl with the fairer skin color would invariably be selected.

A member of the Virginia State College Alumni Association, and also a member of the group which sponsored a choir appearance in Norfolk, asked, "Don't you people up there have any brown-skinned girls who can sing?"

I told her the lighting effects made all the choir members look sort of gray, when they were really of varying shades from white to light brown.

This choir leader was out to raise funds. He wanted to please his public and was thereby catering to what he believed to be the demand. He never sacrificed his musicianship, but nobody recalls even one homely, unattractive headliner in that choir during his tenure.

Being a whole sister myself, I was sorry for this man. My High Priestess insisted we should be proud of our race and proud of ourselves until we ourselves did something to make us hang our heads. I felt then, and I feel the same today, that being a Negro is something to be proud of. I know this man's stupidity hurt the sense of pride and value in some girls, especially girls who had been the leading soloists in their high school choirs, and gave a false sense of superiority to a so-so singer, who made the college choir when she never could make the high school group.

During the second decade of this century the United States Congress passed many bills, urged by the farm bloc in Congress. The Smith-Hughes Act and the Smith-Lever Act had a mighty impact on the schools of the seventeen Southern states. The approval of the Smith-Hughes Act in 1917 marked the beginning of a new policy of the Federal Government toward the financing of education. It started the policy of providing subventions for education lower than the college level.

This act, which is often called the Federal Vocational Education Act, provided money to the secondary schools for instruction in agriculture, home economics, and industrial education. It also provided funds for the preparation of teachers of these subjects.

The money is appropriated to states on the basis of total population, and in order to be eligible to receive these funds, the state or community or both had to spend an equal amount for this work, as well as meet certain other standards prescribed by the act.

The Smith-Lever Act, which became federal law in 1914, is commonly known as the Agricultural Extension Act. It provides federal subventions to aid the states in providing extension work in agriculture and home economics, and was carried on chiefly among adults.

The Smith-Lever Act marked the beginning of the matching principle by the Federal Government.

Although the provisions of these acts specifically refer to the land-grant college of the state, for many years the State of Virginia centered Smith-Hughes work at Virginia State College and Smith-Lever work at Hampton Institute. There were many reasons for this—none, however, that justified this arbitrary use of funds away from the institution specifically designated in the act. (However, Hampton Institute did an excellent job of adult education, lifted the sights of the farmers and their wives, and provided the rural youth with clubs that developed their skills in homemaking and farming.)

At no point in this noble effort was there any thought of integration. The fact that federal funds were involved made no difference. The "separate but equal" cliché was endorsed by the Federal Government. Black heads, hearts, hands, and homes; and white heads, hearts, hands, and homes, for which the 4-H Club insignia stood, were certainly separate and maybe equal.

The fact that Hampton Institute worked with the community, both young people and their parents, proved a distinct advantage in student recruitment. Also, their new campus facilities provided by philanthropists; the response to the Hampton choir, which at one time made a European tour, started the effort to bring the Smith-Lever work to Virginia State College, the land-grant college for Negroes in Virginia.

The shift was made with little dislocation. Miss Lizzie Jenkins, one of the most beloved and respected women in Virginia, who headed the Smith-Lever work with women and girls; and Mr. Patterson, the director of the work with boys and men, moved from the Hampton area to the campus of Virginia State College and operated out of an office there.

Now the work of these two people disclosed to our very own eyes the cries for help from the teacher population, especially from the inadequately prepared teachers in the one-, two-, and three-teacher schools. These were rural schools to which both teachers and children walked many miles through heat, cold, rain, and the occasional snows.

I offered to answer the call. Before this time, I had gone into rural communities to conduct two-day institutes for elementary teachers. In two instances I had conducted six-week summer schools.

Since Virginia had but one state-supported institution for

higher education for Negroes, and that at Petersburg, the vast stretches of land from the tidewater to the Blue Ridge Mountains had no other college, public or private, that offered fully accredited work for public-school teachers. To meet this urgent need, summer schools that could provide an enrollment which would pay all costs of operation, and a registration fee of $3 to Virginia State College for handling grades would be set up on demand. One summer I supervised four six-week summer schools and did full-time teaching in one of them.

Out of these experiences came an awareness of the day-to-day needs of the teachers, the need of the college staff for more information and understanding of the life of the community and also for the patterns of coexistence between the races.

In 1929 the Extension Service at Virginia State College was broadened to include summer services to public-school teachers, which work came under my supervision. I had determined that one way or another the quality of the students being admitted to the college would be improved.

However, turning this New-England-bred city girl loose in rural Virginia almost set back Negro education in that state by another generation. I simply didn't know anything about the farm.

One important lesson learned in the seven years that I traveled over Virginia was that there are many different kinds of knowledge. In some kinds of knowledge I was adept, in others I was abysmally ignorant. In checking a test in which the question was asked, "How many legs has a Guernsey?" I was stumped. I didn't know that a Guernsey was a cow, and I doubt that there was a person in the remotest part of rural Virginia who could not have answered that question.

In Ballsville, Virginia, a dear old soul really gave me my comeuppance.

I was conducting a six-week summer school for thirty teachers at the Ballsville grade school. One afternoon I sat under a beautiful maple tree checking papers while everybody on the farm where I was staying was at work —topping and priming tobacco, picking cherries, or gathering the first beans. I was sitting down and, in the old lady's opinion, doing nothing. She asked me to take some corn to the mules. Sensing her disapproval and wanting to please, I readily agreed.

With my promise to feed the mules, the old lady hurried off about her other chores. Left alone with my problem, I started to reason it out. The cornfield was right beside the house, and I saw no reason to pick the corn and carry it to the mules in the barn. Much more logical, I reasoned, would be to bring the mules out and let them pick their own corn. After much effort, and considerable courage on my part, I led the two mules through the gate and turned them loose in the cornfield.

The old granny must have been looking out the window of the house just then, for she came scrambling out of the house screaming and shouting. Her loud cries drew just about everybody in that hollow to the cornfield. After much effort, the mules were driven out of the cornfield.

With the mules safely returned to the barn—as I later learned so they could not get to water which would have bloated them—the old granny walked right past me on her way back to the house.

"Dang fool woman, can't even feed corn to mules, and her thinkin' she ken teach us somethin'! We's the ones what should be teachin' her!"

For most of this rural schoolwork, the Negro community had to put me up. Usually my abodes were quite poor, inside plumbing was unheard of, and I learned about cold-water cornbread (more water than cornbread). But I was young and strong and didn't complain, and I was a whole sister and these rural people loved me and I loved them.

Our meetings were usually held at the Negro school, and quite often a certain white element would come uninvited and sit in the back rows. They wanted to know what we were up to.

My heart went out to these young girls, struggling their best to be good teachers despite a woeful lack of subject preparation and no teacher-training preparation for their jobs. Yet, in the half-year time allotted them, they were accomplishing surprising results because they knew and understood and loved their children.

One incident, still painful to recall, I believe best sums up why I so willingly gave of my time and myself to these rural teachers.

We were holding a two-day institute. The first morning was cold and snowy, and the wind whistled over the steep foothills of the Blue Ridge. I watched our Negro childen— some of whom had walked five miles—arrive at the one-room schoolhouse. En route these Negro children had been passed up by the district school bus which carried the white children to their school. But my children had walked right on in the belief that what they would learn would break their serfdom to the fields.

I was staying with a family in a little dogtrot cabin.

That night as we stood waiting our turns to go to the outdoor privy, the old-before-his-years head of the little family said, "Miss Butler, long as I kin remember, we been climbing on the rough side of the mountain, climbing up and falling back, and grabbin' bottom. I ain't never been out of sight of that blue mountain yonder, but I figures somewhere there's something better 'n this. I want my young 'ens to get there, Miss Butler. Don't matter me none if those white childrens rides the bus and my kids gotta walk, long as I knows they's getting the education they's going to need. See what I means, Miss Butler?"

Fortunately the darkness hid my moist eyes. That night, as we all tried to sleep in one room, I lay awake and prayed for an answer. I knew these short clinics made good bureaucratic reports, and perhaps gave a little encouragement to some of these young teachers, and the summer schools were a real help, but by no stretch of the imagination could I honestly say that I had upgraded educational standards. And hardest of all to accept, next to the faith of these children and their parents, was the willingness, even eagerness, of most of these rural teachers to learn.

The next day one of the teachers herself provided me with the answer.

"Miss Butler," she said, "problem is we don't have enough background to give these kids what they need. None of us got more than a temporary teaching certificate. Not much chance we'll ever be able to pass the state examination for a permanent three-year teaching certificate."

"What would you do with a permanent certificate?" I asked her.

"Well, it pays more an' maybe I could save enough money to go back to school. With a permanent certificate I could request a leave of absence. Maybe I could go to that school where you teach, and then you'd have time to show me what I need for this job. Do you think I could go to your school, Miss Butler?"

I knew what she meant. Her appearance and manners would be a bit rustic for Petersburg, but if she had that much drive and determination to get a decent education, I knew she would make it. In the following weeks I talked to these rural teachers about certification, regular certification, and what it would do for them. Then I advised them all that I would come back for six weeks that summer and teach them a preparatory course for taking the state certification examination.

Their response was tremendous, and for half a dozen years I gave up most of my summer vacation to help these rural teachers. We could accomplish a great deal in six weeks of concentrated work, and all of these teachers did pass their state certification examinations. Furthermore, they did have their additional income, and they did request leaves of absence and come to Virginia State College to take advanced work. Over the years I have taught the daughters of many of those rural teachers, and even many granddaughters, and perhaps that is why the Negro teachers of Virginia elected me the first woman president of the Virginia State Teachers Association.

Teaching these summer courses did cut down on my time at Newport with my family, but I got home for several weeks each summer and I always went back for my mother's birthday.

All of my brothers and sisters had become wage earners. We had good salaries and were determined that our mother was going to live the good life without worry or concern about money, and therefore everyone of us sent money home. I sent Mother fifty dollars a month, with strict orders to spend the money on herself or keep it in her pocket as she chose.

Once when I was home, Mother took me aside. "Rose," she said, "I don't know about you sending me all that money each month. I was reading where Dorothy Dix says that children shouldn't support their parents but live their own lives. She called it cutting the apron strings."

I just sat her down.

"Now, Frances, you listen to me," I said. "You worked around the clock and denied yourself even the essentials to feed me, clothe me, and teach me. You never complained or ran out of love. Now nothing has ever pleased me as much, from the time I took my first job, as when I gave you the money I have earned. Now just because your needs aren't quite so pressing, don't try to rob me of my present joy of helping you."

While in Newport on this visit, I learned that some of the Jewish children with whom I had shared the lunch hour at Rogers High School, whose families had been just as poor as the Butlers, were now by comparison fairly well off. For the most part, their parents had come from eastern Europe and had known that regardless of how poor they were, they had to save part of what they earned. When money is that dear it is well invested because one will work night and day to make the investment pay off.

It dawned on me that in most instances the Negro does not have the ability to sacrifice that the Jews do. Even today, getting a car is more important to the Negro than getting a house or fixing a leaking roof if he does have a house. If the Negro woman's taste calls for a center cut of ham, and

ham costs $1.50 a slice, she'll buy it even if she lives in a
rented room and winds up with no money left to pay the rent.

The Negro simply hasn't learned to sacrifice. He wants
everything at once, now!

Of course, this started me thinking about my rural teachers
who were making a sacrifice, who were saving their money.
That is when I learned that people with objectives, with
purposes which compel and challenge, will make sacrifices.
Too many of my children simply never have reached a sufficiently high level of experience in a competitive society
to visualize clearly the meaning of life objectives. Without
such objectives there can be no sacrifice.

I recognized that in the future training of teachers of Negro children, we would have to emphasize their involvement
in American life in such a way that the Negro youth would
rise above resentment and honestly feel there was a place
for them in America's emerging industrial society. Their
future employment would have to be at any level at which
they themselves had made the sacrifice to become highly
qualified.

Thus, during those years that I taught my summer
courses, a change occurred in my own awareness of how to
attack the problem of improved education for the Negro and
the poor. You still taught subject content, but your presentation must be one to motivate children and adults to want to
learn. Call it child psychology, for even the poverty area's
adult-child will initially find his motivation on the uncom-
plicated side, perhaps with such a simple stimulus as being
loved, and knowing it.

While explaining this in a workshop one summer, I found
myself in quite an argument with the principal of a nearby
Negro grade school. The man was also a Baptist minister,

for in those days this dual relationship, minister and school principal, was not at all uncommon, although I personally frowned on the practice.

Since obviously we were not going to agree and I wanted the class to get on to other subject matter, I advised this argumentative member that I would be glad to continue our discussion after dinner and gave him the name of the family with whom I was staying. I was quite surprised when he showed up in the evening.

To make a long story short, the next summer we were married.

Someone said, "The Reverend E. T. Browne doesn't have enough education for you, Rose."

I replied, "I'm marrying a man, not his education. Besides, I've got enough education for both of us."

So in the summer of 1929, I became Mrs. Rose Butler Browne. I continued teaching at Virginia State College, and my husband took pastorates as close to Petersburg as possible, enabling me to get home most weekends. If my High Priestess, who had been upset when I hadn't joined the church at eleven years of age, could have seen me now, she would have been proud.

Of course, in the church we dealt with the same people— poor, superstitious, resentful, in need of love, attention, and hope. I left the adults to my pastor husband and concentrated on the children in our Sunday schools. But even here, you had to contend with the adults, as I learned through the following incident, which happened to me at one of my husband's churches.

Although not a member of Pastor Browne's church, this particular family lived near the parsonage and I knew them by sight. They were an emotional family and belonged to a religious sect, one of those where the preacher rears back and squalls and fires the enthusiasm so that the congregation members fling out their arms and dance in the aisles, praising the Lord. However, nobody can remember what the message was about.

One Saturday morning the mother of this family and her two daughters came to visit me. The woman knew that I taught at the college and she let it be known that she had an intense desire for her two daughters to get a college education, although the family had absolutely no money.

The two girls had barely maintained average marks at their secondary school, but they were personable and seemingly bright girls. Considering the family's rural background and the disorganized home environment, I suppose the girls had actually done surprisingly well.

Therefore, I agreed to seek work grants for both girls at a college which I thought might accept them. I also promised to enroll the girls in one of the chaperoned groups of Negro college students who go north each summer to wait table and do housekeeping chores at summer resorts.

I explained that the combination of summer jobs and work grants would provide a bare minimum of needed money. Since the work loads would be burdensome and time-consuming, I predicted this might affect the girls' academic performance. I advised them that when pressures mounted they should take fewer courses per year and extend the time necessary to secure sufficient credits for graduation.

The gratitude of the mother and the two girls was overwhelming.

I had something planned at the college the following weekend, which necessitated my staying in Petersburg, and it was two weeks before I again got home. Right away the mother of the two girls came over. She was alone, but obviously quite pleased with herself.

First she thanked me for my willingness to help her daughters go to college, but advised me that the girls no longer needed my help. She said that she had decided to send her girls to a different school, where they would be making other arrangements than those I had outlined for earning the necessary school funds.

In view of both the academic and home background of her daughters, I did not consider the new school suitable for her girls from either an educational or social standpoint, so I inquired why this particular school had been chosen.

"Why," the woman replied, "they got R.O.T.C. at that school. The Federal Government in Washington pays money to them R.O.T.C. students."

I explained that girls did not take R.O.T.C.

She was appalled that someone who taught at the college did not comprehend her meaning.

"But my girls kin earn that R.O.T.C. money with their bodies," she said. "God give 'em their bodies, didn't he? God will know why they have to do this, so He'll forgive 'em. Jest ain't no other way for my girls to go to college. Didn't seem right for my girls to do all that hard work you was talkin' about. Not when they kin get their college education quicker this way."

Probably, after our first meeting, the two girls had done some thinking about the hard work I had mentioned, and had rebelled over such a work program. Their objectives for going to college were not sufficiently clear for them to look favorably upon such personal sacrifice. After all, it was the mother, not the girls, who had decided they should attend college. So I suppose the mother had then thought up this new scheme, after hearing some gossip over the backyard fence, and had herself rationalized this justification.

Now that was thirty years ago, and with all of today's emphasis on sex, on movies, on TV, in advertisements and in magazines and newspapers, is it any wonder that the poverty areas have a slightly distorted view about sex? At the time this happened, I could not help but compare this home with my girlhood home in Newport. In those days, if an unwed girl was going to have a baby she was sent to a state institution up the Pawtucket River, and there she had her baby and there she stayed for quite some time to work off the expenses.

Today the boys will say of a girl, "She's dead ready," but in my youth in Rhode Island someone was certain to warn such a girl, "You do, and up the river you go."

No member of the Butler family was ever involved with the law, but that did not stop my father from saying to us girls, "You disgrace me and I'll personally break every bone in your body."

Sex education in our home meant you operated within the code, and the code was clearly stated.

Once when the High Priestess was living, we were discussing a neighborhood girl who had been sent up the Pawtucket River. Word had reached us that the girl had had her baby and then placed the child for adoption. The High Priestess was horrified.

"How can she give away her own flesh and blood?" my great-grandmother demanded. "It's hers! Her baby! It's wrong for her not to care for and mother her baby. Her family shouldn't let her do this."

Today, some girls are still working their way through

college by this oldest of professions, but I find myself growing old enough to begin to understand youth. The child who makes a mistake must live with that mistake. It doesn't necessarily have to mean "a life up the river." This is when an errant child needs more love and forgiveness than ever before, and needs some adults whose principles are as practical as those of my High Priestess.

What I am saying is this. I am not so much shocked by the actions of our youth as I once was. It is the reactions of the adults, when confronted with these problems of youth, that appall me.

Now ever since I started teaching at Virginia State College I have found young people who had special needs which I personally wanted to help them meet. Mostly these students were intelligent, quick to learn, eager to learn, but somewhere in their background a hole in their environment had left no one who cared, or taught them self-discipline, or challenged them to take honors by honest effort rather than by less desirable ways. Often their poor grooming and manners blotted out the picture of their intelligence. I found jobs for some of these students; I advanced the money and bought them proper clothes; I taught them cleanliness and pride in appearance; I invited them to dinner parties and spent hours rehearsing them in simple etiquette.

Some of my colleagues joined me in these efforts, including my boon companion, Marguerite Lingham Worthington, who had been graduated from Brown University, Providence, Rhode Island. Marguerite had traveled the same road that I had traveled: hard work, rigid discipline at home, and in addition she had lost her own mother in her early childhood.

Marguerite would always help me with any undertaking for an able and needy youngster. However, when she thought

I was going too far she would lecture me first, and then help. Before too long, she too began to promote the development of promising students, and in some instances I would laughingly accuse her of outmothering me.

These young people who came under our influence might, without this special consideration, have been graduated from college, but would not have taken from that college life the self-confidence and personal pride and firm bearing so necessary to build an academic background into a successful career.

I refer to these students as "my children," and currently have three of them living in our home. I do not know for a certainty how many such students there have been over my nearly fifty years of teaching, but I can safely say the number exceeds two hundred. I am proud of all of my children. However, let me tell you of one boy, Boston Red.

My aunt Lill in Boston had advertised for a chauffeur, and Boston Red had answered the advertisement. He had gotten some money and had purchased a chauffeur's cap. Unfortunately, he had not bothered to get either a chauffeur's license or driver's license, although he had a learner's permit. He assured my aunt that he was a good driver but had lost his references. He was a most convincing talker, and my aunt said she would try him. I was in Boston in summer school at the time, and Aunt Lill was to drive me to Newport.

We drove along on this warm and pleasant Sunday, leaving early so that we would have a full day with my mother. All went well on the way down, but we stayed too long and were on the road home after dark. The long lines of cars coming up from Cape Cod made us move at a snail's pace. Traffic lights were few, but alert traffic officers were posted at intersections. I do not know what happened, but we heard the traffic officer's siren and then he pulled up beside our car and ordered Boston to pull to the side. He called for Boston's driver's license, and the boy brought forth a brand-new learner's permit just two days old. Since I had a driver's license in full force and was on the front seat with him, the requirements of the law were met.

We continued into Boston without further mishap and I offered to help Boston pass the examination for his driver's license. He scorned my offer, but he and his good buddy, Jimmy Smith, managed somehow to get their licenses.

That day, as I listened to and observed that boy, I realized that he was no ordinary young man. He had ability that revealed itself in many ways. He also had a loving family, a father who was a crane operator in the city of Boston, a loving and industrious mother, and a spoiled and unenterprising younger brother. The father loved the boys devotedly. He always bought two chickens, so that each boy could have the part he liked best. In every way he tried to make his boys happy. The mother loved them and was a handmaiden to them. When Boston came home and told her about his new job as a chauffeur, it was she who went dowtown to secure his learner's permit, because the old one had expired.

I learned that the boy was a senior in the High School of Mechanical Arts and a member of the varsity track team with more than ordinary proficiency as a high and low hurdler. The family belonged to the Peoples Baptist Church, and Boston was a regular attendant and active in the young people's organizations.

He had made grades that would keep him in school, but he saw school at this point as a dead end. He finished high school, worked during the summer, and with what help his father could provide, entered Virginia State College in the first year of the great depression.

His name is James Johnson, but his Boston accent, his ability to talk and sell himself and make the best of all situations made him into a campus personality and he became known as Boston Red.

We decided that he should take additional high school work. In a year he finished the college preparatory course at Webster Davis High School and entered Virginia State College as a candidate for a degree in Industrial Arts.

During the depression, in an effort to create jobs, there was new construction on all the college campuses throughout the country. The new building programs at Virginia State College offered a splendid laboratory for the students in Boston's area of training. He had many hours of practical experience in bricklaying, as well as a thorough preparation for teaching of Industrial Arts at the high school level.

While on his first teaching job, Boston Red sent me two masonry flower urns and a bird bath that his students had made. I prize them so highly that these items have made several moves with us and are now part of the scene at our Durham, North Carolina, home.

Once Boston Red called me to say that the principal of the school in which he was teaching wanted him to put his Industrial Arts boys to work making outdoor furniture for the superintendent. Boston didn't think he should do it. I told him to teach the principles involved in making the furniture, guide the students to aim at excellence of performance, and then put the finished product on display at the next P.T.A. meeting. I also advised him to teach two or three boys to explain the blueprints and the selection of materials and to point out the skill in the workmanship. That would be the end of the superintendent's project.

Boston Red talked at length about pussyfooting, etc. I listened until I got tired, since it was a long-distance call with the charges reversed, and brought the conversation to a close.

Some weeks later he called to state that his principal wanted him to have his classes lay a hardwood floor in the auditorium, to help save money for the school board. I said, "Don't you dare undertake to lay a tongue-and-groove floor. First, because you yourself have had no experience in doing a job like that without guidance; second, you cannot teach what you do not know." I reminded him that unborn generations would stumble over that buckling floor to the strains of "Pomp and Circumstance" as graduating classes moved over those lumpy ridges.

He said, "Nobody can guess you. Go ahead and make the chairs. Don't dare lay the floor. What is your story, anyhow?"

He made the chairs but did not lay the floor.

My adult friends at Virginia State College had felt that my boy was most unpromising, although he could outtalk anybody. He talked himself into the second-string varsity football team, warmed the bench for two years, never missed a practice, and made most of the trips. It took him four years to make his varsity letter. As Boston Red was presented the trophy, his voice broke and there were few dry eyes in the gymnasium that night. Persistence and pursuit of excellence had won.

But more than anything my boy wanted to be something big. He wanted to join the Kappa fraternity. He approached me with all kinds of angles, and did he have angles! I didn't budge. One night he came to meet me after dinner and walked with me from the teachers' dining hall singing to me, a little off key, "If you want to go to heaven when you die, you've got to be a Kappa Alpha Psi."

I decided then that being a Kappa meant an awful lot to Boston, because I had told him to stop bothering me about the Kappas. Usually he would not persist when I laid it on the line, so I gave in.

In 1967, when Boston Red and his son both passed the Massachusetts Bar as attorneys, I wanted to put it on the 6:30 P.M. news broadcast. All the people who had thought that I was not too bright in my judgment about my boy didn't know what I knew.

When Elizabeth Sadgwar, also a teacher, came into his life, that was all he needed. His parents with their love and indulgence had prepared him for me, I whipped him into line and got him through school and into a job; Elizabeth brought him happiness.

I am proud of my boy Boston Red. Like most of my children, he is an example of what a little firm love, attention, and patience can mean to an ambitious but uncertain child. Able, determined, but not equipped to face the complicated decisions of our modern society he needed someone—he needed a firm hand to be pulled up by, or to be deflated, as the occasion demanded.

My most precious girl pupil is Ruth. The Master spoke of the one who returned to say thank you. If I were to single out the one who was most appreciative and tried hardest to follow the guidance I attempted to provide, it would be Ruth.

She often reminds me that in her professional life she has always followed my lead. She listened to my guidance at Virginia State College in her undergraduate days. When my husband, whom she affectionately calls "Pop," was called to a church in Bluefield, West Virginia, she came each summer and helped at our house. She attended summer school to strengthen her skills in physical education, art, and music, because her undergraduate preparation was for teaching high school English and she had found employment in the elementary schools. When we transferred to Durham, North Carolina, Ruth came and enrolled in the Graduate School for a Master's degree in Elementary Education. On her commencement day for the Master's degree she said, "Mama, from here on in, I shall be on my own. I am going to get my doctorate by myself without any help from you and Pop."

Ruth still tries to make clear to me that she has a very important private life that has to be lived, and that outside of the professional area I am a first-class "square."

Perhaps one reason for my deepening interest in my acquired children was the fact that my father had died in 1929, and my beloved mother in 1934.

For some time before Mother's death, all of us Butlers had high-paying jobs except Charlotte, who was in training at the Lincoln School of Nursing in the Bronx, New York, and Thelma, who was enrolled in Rhode Island College in Providence, Rhode Island. We children decided that our mother had enough of hard work. I always liked a project, so when eight girls were graduated from Rogers High School in Newport, Rhode Island, who were capable of college admission and in need of assistance, I convinced my mother that we should organize a cooperative housekeeping venture that would make college possible for girls like these. It was a tremendous undertaking. We had to locate a suitable twelve-room house, wheedle my sister Mary and her husband to commute thirty-nine miles to work and arrange all the business aspects.

I took a one-semester leave of absence from Virginia State College to get the project off to a good start. My mother was to be the lady of the manor, my sister Mary was to be the manager and housekeeper, each girl was to carry out assigned duties necessary to a smooth operation. I was to go back to Virginia State for the second semester and send money each month to subsidize the project.

At the end of four years the eight girls were graduated and went in different directions to earn a living and to help other girls make their way through college. My sister Thelma has to this day been engaged in sending promising girls to school and in singing my praise, to my great embarrassment.

When I started my graduate studies at Harvard University, I had to give up reluctantly some of my work with my adopted children as well as my summer preparatory courses for those rural teachers wishing to pass the state certification examination. However, several hundred such teachers had been helped to secure three-year certificates, and thus better-paying jobs, more than a score had already enrolled at the college, and I had confidence the program had opened a way to upgrade these Negro teachers.

My husband was now pastor of a church at Roanoke, in the mountainous section of Virginia, and the school district there asked me to help them conduct a special summer program for Negro pupils. The school board had heard about my summer work in training the teachers of the rural schools. They were anxious to have help for their staff.

It was a most unusual request and so fortunate in its timing that I felt my High Priestess must have been guiding my footsteps. Now I would have complete control of an entire school district for a considerable period of time. I could meet the request of the oral examination committee at Harvard University, for I could set up my control groups in such a manner that there would be no contamination of these pupils through exposure to other reading methods.

I journeyed to Harvard University, and I must state that Dr. Dearborn seemed genuinely pleased and worked quite hard to help me set up my program. Needless to say that was a busy summer.

That fall Dr. Truman Lee Kelly, the statistician from Harvard who had helped me, was visiting at the University of Virginia at Charlottesville. He sent word he would be glad to see me and help with the organization of the statistical data which I had gained from my summer's work.

Dr. Kelly was most helpful, and although not in especially good health at the time, gave of himself unstintingly.

I shall never forget that I was disturbed about not giving I.Q. tests to everyone, and did not know how to report this in my thesis or to the doctorate committee. Since Dr. Kelly had had so much to do with the growth of testing and systems of measurements then in vogue, his answer both amazed and reassured me.

"Mrs. Browne, just omit any reference to the I.Q. tests. If the committee asks, state quite positively there was not time to do everything and you did not consider the I.Q. tests essential under this particular criterion. After all, the I.Q. is merely a relative measure. It shows us what knowledge we have been able to give the child, but does not tell us how much more knowledge the child might have gained by some other environmental conditions. Personally I think you are quite justified in omitting the I.Q. tests."

With the aid of such men, and I must not forget Dr. John

Rothney, then in the Psychology Department at Harvard, I met with my doctorate committee and passed without problems both my oral and written reports.

The results of the experiment indicated that there are no important differences in the effectiveness of the three methods for remedial reading employed in the study, but that each method was effective with some of the children in each group, while other children seemed relatively unaffected, as judged by the scores on the reading test.

However, in these small class groups, with no stigma of being in a remedial reading class, and receiving much teacher praise for their efforts and an occasional ice-cream treat, the result was greater student motivation. We also produced, in each group, an impressive number of significantly higher reading test scores. Thus, from this study, it appeared that remedial reading could be taught in group situations.

In connection with the experiment with ungraded groups of Negro children it should be pointed out that the fact that all the children were Negro children was merely an incident, but it brought into the experimental situation whatever influence race as a factor in learning may carry.

In June of 1937, my husband journeyed to Boston with me and attended the commencement exercises where my Doctorate of Education degree was conferred on me by America's oldest university. My husband was very proud. I want to say that he is an unusual man. Unlike many males who might resent their wife's attaining such high honors, beyond their own attainment, he had pushed me on when I faltered, and now embarrassed me by telling others of my accomplishments. I don't believe I would have persevered without his loyal and wise support.

My own thoughts at the time dwelt at some length on the prophecy of my High Priestess, and on the love of my late mother—yes, even of the loyalty of my father.

That fall I returned to my teaching at Virginia State College and my work there was but little altered, although with my new and more comprehensive background I commenced a much-needed overhauling of our laboratory school program. I wanted to introduce each education major to a great deal more child psychology, more contacts with children, as well as to ways of teaching personal pride in being a Negro.

However, it was in my contacts outside the college, especially in the white educational community, that I met a decided change of attitude.

In those days it had become apparent to both whites and Negroes in the South that times were changing, that our section of the country was but part of a larger social unit. As more members of each race attended the larger universities of the North and Midwest, the blinds of regional myopia fell from many eyes.

In sociology class discussions the white Southerner learned that the rest of the country considered the paradoxes of prejudice a joke, and some of the operational procedures a national tragedy.

Among the paradoxes were these whites who would not sit beside a Negro on a public carrier, but would permit a Negro to cook his food, care for his children—there are reports that Negro mothers were known to serve as wet nurses, who nursed at their own breasts the employers' children. If at a public occasion food was served, there must be no sitting down. If everybody stood up, there was no violation of sacred principles.

This type of behavior was a joke. The Negroes would regale each other with reports of the great lengths to which certain individuals would go to preserve the status quo.

The national tragedies were numerous. The obvious was the impoverished South trying to have two of everything when it could not afford one. Neither the high school for white children nor the high school for Negro children was as good as it could have been, but the idea of one good high school for all children who wanted to go to high school was unthinkable. To mention such an eventuality was treason and meant death or exile, depending on your speed of movement.

The effect of these barriers to communication and easy interaction affected both races. When gatherings for educational purposes threw us together, the Negro members addressed each other as Dr., and added all the sundry titles that pertained. The white members addressed each other as Bill and Jane, but taking the cue, were meticulous in their use of "Mr." and "Dr." when speaking to us.

Today there is some easing up of this silly practice, but I suspect that a grown man who all his life has been referred to by the other race as "boy," or called by his first name, is reluctant to yield his earned prerogatives of title and manhood unless he is sure that there will be a mutual exchange.

A shocker, difficult to absorb, confronts a Negro who in high-level meetings held the trump cards and thereby experienced warm and friendly interaction with other committee members. Outside the committee meeting he might encounter one of the friends of yesterday who stares beyond him without apparent recognition. As a Negro you must recognize that the white is also enslaved by the system. He is friendly toward the Negro cause when he can afford to be;

but at other times you don't embarrass your friend when he doesn't think he can speak to you or recognize your existence and remain in the "in group."

To break some of these paradoxes and tragedies of race may not sound like much, but let me tell you what a forward step it was, for both races were infected by this dry rot. I worked with a Negro County Superintendent who addressed letters to me at the college simply as Rose Browne, Virginia State College. I carefully explained to him that henceforth he should address his letters either to Mrs. Rose Butler Browne or Dr. Rose Butler Browne, that no adult person should be addressed without a proper title.

The man shook his head in bewilderment. "But I want the letters to reach you," he said. "If I put a Mrs. or a Dr. in front of your name, the post office won't know you are colored. They might not know where to deliver the letter."

I told him to try it anyhow, that I was certain the letter would be delivered.

His next letter came addressed to Dr. Rose Butler Browne (colored).

The experience with hidden segregation leaves a mark on both sides of the color line, which it is hard to break.

One of my greatest problems at that time, in the placement of teachers, was matching academic background strengths to job requirements. It was not at all unusual for a teacher who had majored in physical education to be hired by a school district and to find himself, come September, teaching one class in history, one in geography, one in physical education, as well as coaching football, basketball, and track teams, and teaching basketball to the girls.

This situation is still unresolved, although in some sections a teacher is penalized by a reduction in salary if she teaches out of her field. In the early days, the real problem was that the Negro principal was saddled with the responsibility of building a four-year, sixteen-unit, three-teacher high school. Assuming that each teacher had a major and a minor concentration, there were only six disciplines available to him. At this time the basic of nine constants of the high school curriculum comprised four units of English, two units of science, two units of social studies, and one unit of mathematics. The other seven units had to be selected from a distribution of approved courses provided by the State Department of Education.

The state program consisted of eleven grades, seven elementary and a four-year high school, which was the pattern throughout the seventeen Southern states in the schools for both races. In many instances in the Negro schools, the seventh-grade teacher was provided by the parents. Sometimes her total salary for the eight-month term (which became standard during the fourth decade of the century) was provided by the parents. In other instances the county, with the assistance of the state, provided salary for seven months and the parents paid for the eighth month and in more progressive districts for the ninth month.

Often the strength and energy of the teachers were so completely drained by the money-raising activities that the teaching suffered. Often the parents who were spearheading the drives left the programs, festivals, "sellings," and other devices to the imagination of the teachers. Occasionally some of them must have realized that they were being "had."

For example, one popular money-raising device was a pie walk. The parents would bake twenty-five pies, which would be on display the night of the fund raising. Under each pie the teacher would place a number, corresponding to num-

bers 1 to 25, which were written on the assembly floor and
circled. For ten cents a person could enter the pie walk. When
twenty-five persons had paid their dime, the walk on the
circles would begin. At a given signal all walkers would stop
on whatever circle they were on. A child would then lift a pie
and the person standing on the circle with the matching number would receive the pie. Another pie would be substituted
and the walk would continue until all the pies were disposed
of at $2.50 each, or until no more walkers could be en-
ticed to participate. Then the teacher who had charge that
night might turn saleslady and try to dispose of the remaining pies for $1.00 each.

The parents would provide the pies and then come to the
festival and buy them back in the name of education.

As the move for state accreditation intensified the need
for the standard eight-month term, a faculty of at least three
teachers, each of whom held a baccalaureate degree, some
semblance of a library, science equipment to support the
science offerings, and separation of the elementary and high
school faculties in teaching assignments became necessary.
This all meant that the beleaguered principal was indeed hard
pressed. Failure to provide a full high school program would
mean that he would soon be replaced, for the parents would
go to the County School Board and complain. Since no one
was concerned about the quality of the work, and many of
the teachers involved in these intolerable conditions had received their own training under similar or harsher conditions, they had to put their hearts into the teaching and their
shoulders to the money-raising wheel. They prepared many
students who went off to Virginia colleges to repeat one or
two grades of high school work before becoming college
graduates of more than ordinary stature.

I can think of the Morgan children from Dilwyn in Buckingham County, who attended four and five months of elementary school, entered the high school department of Virginia State College, went on to college, and earned honors as they progressed. All of the Morgan children hold Master's degrees today. However, they did use extraordinary judgment in selecting their mother and father.

In the early winter of 1939 my husband accepted a pastorate at Bluefield, West Virginia. This coal-mining community in the southern part of the Mountain State is the site of Bluefield State College, and I applied for a teaching position, hopeful that my husband and I might at last work in the same community. The college responded by offering me a fine position, although I had to wait almost a year until my contract at Virginia State College had been fulfilled.

I had been at Virginia State College for seventeen years and left there with a good feeling. Much of my educational training was visible in the curriculum, in the cultural programs, in the upgrading of the education of teachers in the state. Virginia had been good to me, and I would miss my many friends, but my husband was in West Virginia and the situation at Bluefield State College was one to challenge my abilities.

I had gone to Virginia State College eager to teach and had put all that I had into my work. In the early years, while I was getting my bearings, the chairman of the department, a Fisk University graduate, gave me what would be described today as an internship in teaching. I could not describe to her my deep frustration because it was many years later that I found out what it was. I was attempting to draw on experiences that I assumed that my students had had. I based my assumptions on their chronological ages and years of school.

Until I began my work with the rural teachers and lived in their homes and became one of them, I did not know how different were their environmental resources from what I knew. I was to learn that their environment had more in it than had ever been utilized.

However, Miss Colson was my guide and inspiration in those early years as she touched my life, and I still call her friend. Now she is Dr. Colson and has been retired many years, but she still maintains a deep interest in the world around her.

Chapter 6

WEST VIRGINIA

During my last semester at Virginia State College my interest was divided between the building of a new home in Bluefield, West Virginia, and rounding out my career at my first teaching position.

My husband had found a suitable lot in a neighborhood not too far from the center of town and bordering on the middle-class white community. For the most part the people on Ellis Street held membership in the Scott Street Baptist Church, to which my husband had been called as pastor.

Scott Street Church was an old-line church. The members were financially secure home owners and knew the niceties of daily living. They were not members of the learned professions, but they earned good salaries working in the mines and on the railroads. The men were the wage earners; few, if any, women worked.

When my husband interviewed the owner of the land, an elderly lady, she agreed to sell the lot for cash. "I don't want any notes," she said. "I want cash money!"

On the appointed day my husband met her in the lawyer's office with a cashier's check for the stipulated sum. The owner, who had grown up in the traditional master-servant relation with Negroes was astounded when she saw the cashier's check.

She said, "Preacher, where did you get all this money?"

"My wife and I worked for it."

"What are you going to do with all that land?" she asked.

When he told her that we were going to build a house and landscape the grounds, she said, "Well, well, well, did I ever. . . . Will you let me come and see your house when it is finished?"

It had been my hope that I would come from Virginia State College directly to our new home, but this was not to be. The weather, the power structure, the many irritations and delays contingent to cutting down a mountainside, building eleven-foot rock walls to retain the mountain; paying to have loads of dirt hauled away and then paying to have less fertile soil hauled back to build a lawn all contributed to the delays.

I recall talking to a member of the Deacons' Board who declared that he had never heard tell of honest folks building a house like that without asking somebody to go on a note. His parting comment was that it was none of his business where we got all that money; it wasn't even his business whether or not we were honest. I did not tell him that we had sold a house in a most affluent section of Richmond adjoining the campus of Virginia University for more money than the Bluefield house cost. However, he reputedly told some members of the church, "We got a good pastor, but a woman with all that learning ain't going to help him none—her talking to me like I was another woman."

On the fifteenth day of August, 1940, we spent the first night in our new home. Every piece of furniture was in place and the house was a thing of beauty. The Richmond house was more imposing, but it was already built when we bought it. This house had been designed with each line expressing our wishes. Each piece of furniture was chosen for the spot in which it was placed, or the spot was chosen for the furniture.

I was home at last. I would live at home and work in the same community as my husband. Right then I put down my roots. I said to myself, "This is it, girl. Bluefield is home."

There was real joy as we moved into that remarkable clean freshness of a brand-new house, a house we had put so much of ourselves into in the planning and execution. Only those who have delighted in such an experience can know my sense of pleasure. A woman with a home and children and a loving husband is indeed rich.

Our home had a large grassy yard bordered with bright flower beds. A massive carpet of blue morning glories climbed over the rocky walls of the mountain which towered above the back of our lot. The most relaxed moments of my life were spent sitting by that spring, beneath the blue morning glories, watching my husband putting out fruit trees and planting grapes.

While we were still busy planting flowers and getting settled in our new home, a friend of mine from West Virginia State College at Institute, West Virginia, came to persuade me to take his place at West Virginia State for a semester. This friend had taken a year's leave of absence to complete work on his doctorate at Northwestern University,

Evanston, Illinois. However, his major professor had told him, at the close of the summer session, that he would have to return to Northwestern for another semester.

President John Davis of West Virginia State had told my friend he could not release him for a semester unless he could find someone of equal or better training than his, who would be willing to come for the semester he would have to miss. My friend had taken his family to Evanston, Illinois, for two years, and funds were an item with him. I knew there would be some delay in my appointment to Bluefield State, so reluctantly I agreed to go the 130 mountain miles to help this colleague.

Once the decision was made, I looked forward to the privilege of working with Dr. Davis and Mr. James Evans, as well as the association with my many friends at Institute.

Soon after I got my program of work under way, I became aware that something was different about me physically. All my life I had jumped out of bed in the morning as though starting a track event. Now, some mornings when I had a ten o'clock class, I would miss breakfast and sleep. And so, after eleven years of married life, I learned that I was pregnant.

Actually, I rather enjoyed the semester at West Virginia State, though there was nothing else to compare that school with Virginia State. These two Negro universities were quite different. There was more culture and educational depth and mission to uplift the student level at Virginia State; but under Dr. Davis, more pupil freedom and dynamic political challenge existed at West Virginia State. Provocative speakers were brought to the Sunday-night student forums, speakers who covered the political, economic, racial, and social problems of the nation, as well as those persons who spoke on more academic subjects. However, the forum idea was not limited to Sunday nights. All over that campus, often under guidance of a faculty member, little islands of students gathered and regularly debated pertinent topics of the day.

I found myself in a remarkably alive atmosphere, argumentative and searching. Often these arguments got out of hand, and seldom could they be referred to as genteel in their decorum, for these students were probing the domestic issues of their times and evaluating the gap between America's promise of equal citizenship for all and her performance toward colored people.

West Virginia State College also had a progressive Trades and Industries Division which met a great need by providing marketable technical skills for many students to whom the purely academic was neither challenging nor attainable.

The student body at the two state universities differed, just as did the schools themselves. Yet, I dare say the authorities at each school knew that, despite all the academic, technical, and special contacts offered, the baccalaureate found them graduating many students not yet ready for the competitive world where they had to earn a living.

These were especially exciting times at West Virginia State College. In the northern part of the state were located many defense plants, especially in the production of synthetic rubber and plastics. Graduates and instructors from the chemistry department of both Bluefield State College and West Virginia State College were in considerable demand for this work force. The college chemistry professors were called in for special work assignments in the laboratories of the plants.

The working force in these new chemical plants represented a real mixture of nationalities, chief of which were recently arrived South European immigrants. These workers, not yet restricted by any racist viewpoint, observed these Negro chemistry professors holding down good jobs in the laboratories. They recognized this required ability, and they would comment among themselves, "That fellow is smart. I want my son to study under him at his college."

As a result, near the close of the war, our first white students—medically discharged service men and often sons of these South European workers, enrolled at West Virginia State College, previously and by practice an all-Negro school. There were no student problems because these white boys came with a specific purpose in mind, to learn chemistry or related technical skills. Just as long as they were busy learning a marketable skill, no time remained for racial friction.

Their presence had a startling effect on the Negro students. The fact that these white boys had voluntarily selected West Virginia State College gave the Negro students some pride in their school, in their faculty, in the offered curriculum program. It did something wonderful to the student self-image, for here was proof of the worthwhileness of their college and its training.

However, there also was an amusing negative side. The Negro students protested that their professors were now loading on the homework just to impress the white boys and their parents.

What started near the end of the war years has continued in West Virginia, both at Bluefield State College and at West Virginia State College, where I understand today there are more white than Negro students. When you are poor and seek an education, the goal of education comes first, ahead of such wasteful distractions as race and nationality hatreds.

In January, at the close of the first semester, I left Institute and went back over Flat Top Mountain to enjoy my new home and to argue with my husband on the relative value of boys and girls as offspring. He wanted a son and I wanted a girl.

The whole Butler family got into the act. My brother John had nine children. Among the other Butlers, five girls and another boy, there was but one child.

My friends and former students from Virginia sent so many and such fine gifts that I gave the things I had purchased to the "poor," and prepared for the young prince or princess in the style to which he was to become accustomed.

My sister Thelma, who was teaching at Winston-Salem State College, in Winston-Salem, North Carolina, came up to be with me and stayed until she had to leave for summer school.

Among those who came to help was Mrs. Julia Cooper, a teacher in the Roanoke, Virginia, city school system, whose daughter and son were my contemporaries. Believe me, no eastern potentate had more fanfare to announce his arrival than our son Emmett. Little Jimmy Seay, who lived on the other side of Ellis Street, was heard to scream, "Mama, here comes Miss Browne and *our* baby!" Little E. T. was made welcome to the Ellis Street community.

In September I became a member of the faculty of Bluefield State College. I was warmly welcomed by the dean of the college, with whose sister I had worked for all the years I was at Virginia State, and by Professor S. L. Wade, a graduate of Brown University in Providence, Rhode Island, who was also a member of my husband's church.

The president of the college, Dr. H. L. Dickason, was one of the most sincere men that it has been my experience to meet. He had a childlike faith in the integrity of men. He had served as dean under the preceding president and felt that men would deal with him as he had dealt with his superior. West Virginia was and still is a state in which political influence has always been strong. Regardless of the "in" party, "Old Hickory" taught them well that to the victor belongs the spoils. Dr. Dickason ran the college honestly and sincerely and a little late learned of the perfidy of men.

One of the desires of his heart was full accreditation for Bluefield State College. Dr. John W. Davis, the president of West Virginia State College, had led that college to full accreditation in the North Central Association, which made it the only West Virginia state college primarily for Negro students to be accredited.

Bluefield State College's catalog stated that it had a B rating with the American Association of Teachers Colleges. A representative from that association demanded that the statement concerning the B rating be removed from the college catalog. Everyone knew how this news would affect the college enrollment.

A committee headed by the dean of the college set out to seek accreditation, but met with no success. I asked President Dickason if he really wanted the school accredited. He said that he wanted it more than anything else. I asked him to announce that he had given me the assignment and I would draw on my years of experience at Virginia State and my previous experience with the accrediting association. I also requested members of the faculty who were able and willing to help.

Without fanfare, Mr. Felbert Dunlap and other staff members, Dean Whiting, and Mr. C. W. Browne, the registrar of the college, worked with me on the standards of accreditation. There is nothing mysterious about accreditation. The standards are written in simple, straightforward language, and you soon know whether or not your college is in full achievement, working on the standard, or not yet ready.

We had a visitation committee at the college and were given full accreditation. Dr. Dickason was very appreciative of the leadership which I had given and rewarded me with a sizable raise in salary.

Soon after this, Dr. Dickason received an honorary doctorate at Virginia State College. Those men at Virginia who had worked with Dr. Dickason at Bluefield were proud of the recognition for a man who had dealt honestly with them. I was proud to recommend him to the Committee on Honorary Degrees, and prouder still that not one dissenting voice was raised when his name was presented to the large faculty of that college.

As Christmas approached that year, I decided that now we were a family we should celebrate this holiday like the big and glorious Christmases I remembered from my childhood.

My husband came from a very poor family. As a boy, he would be given his shoes for the winter just before Christmas. At Christmas he usually received one candy cane and one gingerbread man. His concept of family gatherings, of festive occasions, was sketchy, but I made up for this deficiency. I knew what to do and laid my plans along memory's guidelines as I recalled those wonderful festive Butler Christmases in Malden and Boston and Newport.

Since the stores in Bluefield were limited in their merchandise selections I drove to Lynchburg, Virginia, one Saturday to go shopping. In one of the department stores a little Negro boy, crying as though his heart would break, literally ran into me.

He started to pull away, but I held out my arms and he flew into them. I asked if I could help, but he sobbed all the louder.

"There must be some reason for your tears," I said.

"Santa Claus shook everybody's hand, but he wouldn't shake mine," he sobbed.

The lad was not much older than my little Emmett, and my heart went out to him. A padded Santa Claus who didn't believe in the Preamble of the United States Constitution, or in the 13th Amendment to that document, had just told this child the awful truth that life for him in America would be different—even his dream of Santa Claus had to go.

I thought of going to the department store head, but instead told the lad I had a little boy just like him, that I had been shopping and thought if we looked through my purchases we might find a present he would like. Before we had finished searching my purchases, his tears had stopped. Finally, with a toy clutched in his hand (and a purchase receipt in his pocket) he left me. He thanked me and tried bravely to smile and then ran out through the crowd of busy white Christmas shoppers.

I recall another Santa Claus incident, which occurred at a Negro church. Santa Claus had been late arriving and had put on the traditional uniform quite hurriedly. He had handed out only two or three presents when a little girl spoke out.

"That's not Santa Claus," she said. "Santa Claus doesn't have black hands!"

This Santa Claus had forgotten to put on his white gloves.

Personally, I feel that racial discrimination has been relegated entirely too long in our national awareness to a twilight zone. Discrimination does exist, and it does hurt my little children, who in a few more years will turn their lives either toward productive or destructive paths—according to what American society has permitted them to build of their dreams.

When I got back to Bluefield after that shopping trip and was within the protective walls of our house, with my son and husband present, I again felt secure. This was our home. It was wonderful to own your own home.

However, on September 24, 1947, while we were getting Emmett ready to attend his first-grade class, the telephone rang. My husband had been called unanimously to the pastorate of Mount Vernon Baptist Church, Durham, North Carolina. He was elated about going, but I was crushed, and quite positive that I would not leave my dream house and the job I so enjoyed.

Just then things commenced happening so fast that I hardly had time to think of my own problems. Near the end of October, Dr. James E. Shepard, the founder and president of North Carolina College in Durham, died. On November 6. I went to Petersburg for the funeral of Dr. John M. Gandy, president emeritus of Virginia State College. On November 7, my husband, Emmett, and I made our first visit to Durham as a family. We worshiped at Mount Vernon Baptist Church on November 8 and met some very kind and lovely people.

My husband moved about among these people as if he belonged there. I told myself he was acting as though he had forgotten that young orchard that he had set out at Bluefield before Emmett was born. Besides the orchard there were the five kinds of grapes that he had always wanted to try out, and those big fat hens and turkeys. When I reminded him of these past projects, he was all smiles. "I'll have everything straightened out," he said. "I have until the first of the year."

He did, too. He killed and sold the chickens and turkeys, and the fruit that was not gone was shared or stored.

My sister Thelma, who had spent Christmas with us, drove with us to Durham, where we were to spend the week-end and New Year's Day. We had a wonderful time. The members extended themselves on our behalf. On New Year's Day Thelma returned to Winston-Salem, my husband remained in Durham, and little Emmett and I left by train for Bluefield. We were due to arrive at Bluefield at 8:45 P.M., but finally got in around midnight. A heavy snow had all but buried the town. Deacon Kenner had the house warm, the snow removed from around the walks, and he met us at the station.

En route home we had picked up Fannie, my current adopted child, who lived with us while attending school. As the three of us sat in the house feeling somewhat awed and alone after Brother Kenner left assuring us he would return, my small son looked up at me and said, "Mother, you and Fannie have to mind me because Daddy said I'm the man of this house while he's away."

I assured Emmett that he was welcome to his role as I felt most inadequate at that minute.

The next day the gods started ganging up on me. The streets became so icy and snow-choked that walking was difficult. When I moved to West Virginia, I had been leery about driving in the mountains and had permitted my driver's license to lapse; besides, we had only one car and it

was with the pastor in North Carolina. I had to haul
groceries and our laundry on Emmett's sled. To add to the
general confusion, that young man had to get on the sled
with the groceries or laundry because he was the man of
the house and Daddy had said we were to mind him. Fannie
pushed and I pulled, and we accomplished our operations
in spite of the master of the house.

I could not "bop" Emmett because his Daddy was the
culprit; and I could not tongue-lash his daddy because in
all of our reports we said we were getting on beautifully.

Meanwhile I had plenty to think about. I didn't want to
leave my home, but with my husband away, Fannie in her
senior year, the six-year-old man of the house, and the bitter
winter, I was weakening at the seams. We were cold all the
time. We would bank the fire at night, start it up in the morning, bank it when we left for school, start it up when we came
home after school. When the house had just about warmed
up again, it was time to bank the fire for the night.

One evening when I was bathing my little boy, he said,
"Mommy, this world is real cold since Daddy went away,
isn't it?"

I said, "It's just beginning to warm up."

No more banking fires. I kept stoking coal, and Fannie
hauled ashes. Before spring we had burned twenty tons of
coal, but we were warm, and coal was cheap in West Virginia. I was working and Daddy was sending us money
every month.

Besides not wanting to leave our home in Bluefield, my
other reason for not wanting to go to North Carolina was
my reluctance to teach in a situation I felt to be negative.
Teaching at North Carolina College under Dr. Shepard
would have been difficult. He had invited me to join the

faculty some years before, but did not offer enough money to warrant my leaving Virginia State College. However, I had been challenged by his dedication and sense of sacrifice for the education of the youth of his race.

Dr. Shepard was a graduate pharmacist, in which profession he could have made a good living. He was a finished and polished orator who knew exactly how to turn a phrase. In fact, his very appearance—handsome, tall, well-proportioned physically, impeccable in his dress—spoke of a leader.

However, he believed what he believed, and no one could seriously challenge his beliefs. For example, when he was directed to offer graduate work at North Carolina College, he went to the University of North Carolina and to Duke University and employed white teachers in the graduate schools of those institutions to carry out the program. When criticized, he told the critics to find him some Negro teachers of like experience and eminence and he would employ them. I was not a member of the faculty under Dr. Shepard, but am of the opinion there were some eminent scholars who warranted a greater display of his confidence.

In the matter of salary, Dr. Shepard's pay scale for six weeks' summer school was $500 for a white professor with a doctorate and $250 for a Negro professor with the same academic preparation.

The fact that this policy existed indicated to all that Dr. Shepard believed it was right. He made no effort to deceive anyone. He offered you what he was going to pay you and you could take it or leave it. The white people were used to tide the college over a difficult period.

On the thirtieth of January, 1948, Dr. Alphonso Elder, who had been dean of the Undergraduate College and Dr. Shepard's right-hand man, was named president. I had known Dr. Elder from my Virginia days and knew he had a real interest in the total development of students.

When my husband had first told me he was going to Durham, I had said he would have to go without me. He had replied, "Woman, when you married me you knew that I considered myself called of God. I feel that God wants me in North Carolina. I am going. Now I would hate to lose you, but you will have to decide that."

That decision was being hastened by the snow and cold, by stoking the furnace, and then by the heavy rains which washed down the mountains. I found myself thinking that Durham might not be too bad, and with someone I knew leading the college, I might even change my mind.

Eighteen days after Dr. Elder's appointment as president I sat in his office and talked over possible employment. At the close of that conference, I had agreed to join the faculty at North Carolina College at a salary less than I was then earning at Bluefield State, but Dr. Elder was a new president and had not drawn up or presented his budget. Occasionally as we talked, I would glance down at the corns on my hands from stoking that furnace. The chance to live where the winters were mild and short made me willing to accept whatever was offered. I was neither the breadwinner nor the head of the family, and North Carolina was a new area in which I could help children.

Also, I knew that Emmett belonged in Durham with his daddy. Our little family would be together again. With Fannie's graduation assured, my obligation there was fulfilled.

The only remaining impediment to the move was 215 Ellis Street, my dream house, the home to which had brought our newborn son. My husband and I decided not to sell the house but to rent it to a member of the church who was an excellent housekeeper and loved our home as much as we did. It was not hard to leave some of my most precious possessions with Alice and Hannibal Walls, because they were precious people.

At last Emmett and I were ready to join the pastor in Durham.

Chapter 7

NORTH CAROLINA

College

In September of 1948, I started teaching at North Carolina College, and still teach there. These have been years of progress, during which America has undergone basic revisions in its social structure. In no area has this social progress produced more accelerated demands than on the campus of the Negro college. We no longer tutor a silent generation of students. Although our students still come largely from homes which possess few status symbols, these young people today are seized by a raw determination to end their disenfranchisement. The American dream of equal opportunity stirs their emotions. Most would work their hearts out to attain that dream, if convinced our American society will permit them access to positions other than the traditional peasant-peon role of the Negro.

They know all about the Negro's past role in America, and they aren't buying it. They know the awful price.

Although an ineffectual parent, at least my father remained in our home exerting discipline and maintaining order, and my mother and father were together on matters of family action. Today, more than one quarter of all Negro teen-agers come from broken homes in which the father figure is absent. Inquiry reveals that the unemployed father set out to find work elsewhere, but he never came back or sent for his family.

Poverty and aloneness can make a child a realist ahead of his years. These youngsters recognize that in the rough and tumble economics of job competition their fathers had no marketable skills other than the brawn of their sweaty backs. The more perceptive youths generally attribute their father's failure to segregated and inadequate education. This, then, is the new breed of youngsters who come to college with change as their goal, confident that education must be the answer, yet suspicious of the quality of all instruction received.

They arrive at college with the dollar sign as their status symbol and money as their god, and have practically no concept of work as an end in itself. Success is measured by a flashy car and fashionable clothes, and failure means you're back on the street with more despair, more indolence, more poverty, and more bitter resentment.

I do not find youth's attitude strange. In America today many people no longer take any particular pride in their work. Although eager to take longer and longer coffee breaks and indulge in work slowdowns, such persons remain firmly convinced that their American rights assure them of annual pay raises for less and less work, and fringe benefits that will provide this affluent life forever. Should the sons and daughters of America's disenfranchised Negro have nobler ideals and work habits than the franchised race?

Thus it becomes our task at college, particularly the Negro college, to redirect such student attitudes and manners and outlook—in addition to providing basic instruction in the various curriculum disciplines, and keeping such instruction relevant to America's technological advances and needs.

The task is difficult. The problem is compounded by television whose commercial sales pitch is directed at the white middle-class and suburban populace. However, besides the monied primary target, these programs also are seen in the tenements of the inner city and the shacks of rural America. To my knowledge there exists no counterbalance to this picture of national affluence shown repeatedly on the television screen. This is proof positive to the self-willed but experience-restricted youngster of the black community who "knows" that all of America—all except that segregated black portion where he must live—buys a new car each year, lives in modern houses filled with work-saving devices like washers, dryers, and the latest electric ranges, and belongs to families who take a second vacation. The black youngster hasn't had his first "fun" vacation yet, and many will walk the streets in hopeless search of work.

As youth will do, they vow to get hold of the dollars and enjoy their share of the good life. They bring a stubborn resolve to college, but often arrive pathetically ill prepared in academic background and even the elementary social graces. These failures are the product of an ever-widening gap between the level of home life and the quality of institutional services known to the poor and the not-so-poor.

When I read of Negro students in a major city (in this instance a Northern city) forcing a high school principal to resign, my heart goes out to these poor children. The sharper ones have reached an awareness that in that particular school they were getting at best a second-class education. Second class will not suffice today! The demand is for the best. If America fails them, these youngsters will turn to destruction as a means of gaining a measure of control over their seemingly inescapable environment, and as a means of releasing their own pent-up tensions.

Personally, I think we have gained ground in this struggle for basic education; not Negro education, but education for the poor, which includes the poverty areas of all races. I base my opinion as much on the outcry of the extremists of various races, who have become shrill and overzealous, as I do on any statistical compilations.

Now, more than anything else, the Negro college wants the middle class of white America to light a few lamps of hope amidst the darkness. The status quo of American racial segregation has shifted. These changes will progress in peaceful fashion only as preconceived notions about race—notions officially torn asunder by present civil rights laws—are set aside in personal interaction between our black and white societies.

However, the year 1948—when I came to North Carolina College following the death of Dr. James E. Shepard— began a new era in education at that college.

Dr. Shepard's image of a liberal arts college had been eroding for some time. Negro students could ill afford a college education which taught them the life of a "gentleman."

Of necessity, the Negro college student had to be involved in the "bread and butter" concerns of earning a living.

The college's approach to its task sorely needed change. In those days secondary school teaching had become the reluctant but final job choice of a majority of the students. Little else was available. A few, dazzled by the impact of the Durham community (site of the home office of North Carolina Mutual Life Insurance Company, the largest Negro-owned and -operated business in the world) did turn to commercial programs, with insurance the principal area of concentration.

Actually, the students were fortunate, since this liberal arts emphasis gave North Carolina College graduates a better general education program than that found in most colleges within the state, whether they served white or Negro students. The college's failure, however, was to direct its students into fields of special concentration and areas of specific preparation.

At that time North Carolina College offered no majors in the field of education. Its only reason for offering educational courses was to make it possible for students desiring to teach to meet state certification requirements.

In 1948 the college's educational offerings fell into an area for which the dean of the Undergraduate College was assigned responsibility. Earlier, when the administration received the go-ahead for graduate work in elementary education, the need of organization and leadership for such programs demanded change.

Undergraduate programs in elementary education were not included in the offerings of the college, so the library collection in this area had to be started from scratch. Until I joined the staff in 1948, no full-time worker for the area of elementary education had been employed.

The requirement for the Master's Degree was thirty semester hours of graduate work: Three hours for the thesis, from nine to twelve hours in the minor field, and from fifteen to eighteen semester hours for the major field. Up to this time guidelines for the sequence of courses leading to the graduate degree in elementary education had not been set up. I was assigned responsibility for setting up a sequence of courses, planning for library support for the courses indicated, and developing outlines and syllabi for the courses which I should teach. This assignment came from the president.

At this point the undergraduate education program was the responsibility of the undergraduate dean, and graduate programs of education were administered by the absentee dean of the Graduate School.

Dr. Elder next took a bold step to secure more consistent leadership for the college's rapidly enlarging Graduate School. The incumbent dean, a full-time dean of the Graduate School at the University of North Carolina at nearby Chapel Hill, maintained his primary interest there. He was a good man, an eminent scholar, and he served conscientiously despite a well-known weakness.

A young Negro with degrees from Bowdoin College, the University of Iowa, and Harvard University, was appointed the new dean of our Graduate School. While this new man took over his enlarged responsibilities, the former dean came to the campus once a week, as he had always done, and served in an advisory capacity.

As the faculty of the Graduate School was employed, Dr.

Elder wisely presented the idea of having all teachers serve on both the graduate and undergraduate levels in order that students might have a continuing relationship with persons of scholarly outlook. This wise decision helped overcome a previous weakness, an area of great dissatisfaction for those of us responsible for graduate programs.

Formerly, we never knew what graduate courses were to be offered until the dean came over from Chapel Hill, late the afternoon of registration day. Then the dean and the registrar would confer, and not until then were we told what graduate courses we would be teaching. My first semester's program at North Carolina College consisted of fifteen hours of graduate work, spread out from eight o'clock in the morning until nine o'clock at night on different days of the week. It took me a month of scrambling to get my class outlines and library references in shape. My library work in the courses dealing with the elementary school of necessity had to come from periodicals until the books that had been ordered for the library had been received and processed.

Also, attitudes of racial discrimination, when a white teacher would be favored over a Negro teacher of equal training, was soon to become a thing of the past at North Carolina College. No longer would a white teacher who had majored in sociology at the University of North Carolina be paid $750 a semester for each of two 3-semester-hour courses in psychology, while a Negro teaching a full load of five courses of 3-semester hours each (and these in the field of her major concentration) would be paid at the rate of $450 per course taught during the same period.

All of us on the faculty felt the pressures of new standards as our college programs were made more relevant to the practical needs of students.

In the early 1950's a building program at the college brought seven new buildings, including a three-story Education Building designed to serve the immediate and future needs of the department. At this period, I was chairman of the Department of Education, and the planning and equipping of the building was a most stimulating all-department enterprise.

Frances Eagleson, a poised and charming woman, and I met the need for an attractive tearoom (where by example we could teach social graces and manners) by purchasing beautiful draw drapes to cover windows and an entire wall of blackboards. A mirror could be set over the bulletin board, and living-room furniture, lamps, tables, and a soft green rug turned the classroom into a showplace with no arguments from the budget committee.

As a means of strengthening the preparation for teaching, we instituted an integration of courses which made it possible for the seniors in teacher education to remain with the Department of Education. The student entered the program for eighteen weeks. The first two weeks were involved in orientation to the North Carolina school system. The second two weeks were spent living in the school community in which the student was to do his laboratory teaching the second half of the semester. In this period the student observes the classroom teacher, serves as a teacher aide, writes a job description of the teacher's activities, learns the names of the children and seating plan of the classroom. The third period was four weeks of preparation for teaching in the school visited. The methodology was handled by teachers of the specific subject matter; the professional aspects were in the province of education. The professor in the area of administration prepared students to make all state-required reports. The second half of the semester was spent living and working in the community where the original two week period had been spent.

Another old problem had also to be faced. We had a very high percentage of incoming students who needed subfreshman English and mathematics courses. On the faculty a number of us also insisted that students needed to improve their reading skills. The need for such a remedial reading program was clearly demonstrated through substandard performance on entrance tests; the unsatisfactory academic records made by students who came to college ill prepared; and the ever-increasing demands for reading both in college and in later life.

From the hour of its inception the North Carolina College reading-skills program became embroiled in controversy. Was it a credit course or a noncredit course? In which of several departments did it rightfully belong? After a faculty committee investigation the course was left with the Education Department as a noncredit course. However, the president of the college expanded the reading emphasis to include what he called "A Supervised Program in Pleasurable Reading." The students quickly tagged the course "Compulsory Joy."

Most students in this course had never learned to meet the reading demands of a college. They hated reading with a lively passion and attempted only the required reading in their school courses, for the most part factual reading, and they did as little of that as possible.

Such students came from homes where reading material

was quite limited. Undoubtedly they also came from schools where each September the second-grade teacher would tear her hair and in a rash of self-pity would protest, "Look what the first-grade teacher sent me. These children can't read!" She would complain without realizing that the teaching of reading does not stop with the first-grade basics, but continues on and on throughout our entire life.

These young people also reflected a lack of exposure to children's libraries, or else the tragic situation of insufficiently trained library staffs and limited budgets for purchasing books.

The "Compulsory Joy" program proposed to motivate such freshmen and sophomore students by having them read a minimum of six books for pleasure during the academic year. To this end, several thousand dollars were invested in paperback books.

Paperback books were selected for a number of reasons. They have the modern twentieth-century look, are reasonably priced, and offer a wide variety of topics and writing styles. In the minds of these poor readers the paperback book unquestionably has a less formidable appearance than most hard-cover books. To further the concept of reading for pleasure, the books were displayed in magazine racks similar to those found at the popular corner drugstores.

To ensure that the students actually read the books, and not just a summary, oral tests were designed. I of course recalled from my childhood how our Boston librarian would ask me, "Now Rose, what does this book tell about? Would you like to read me a little of what you most enjoyed?"

The Pleasurable Reading Program, now in operation for more than a decade at North Carolina College, has been broadened to include all departments and their lists of books.

Titles dealing with African history, Negro life and literature, and some of the older religions remain extremely popular with our college readers.

The program is designed not only to help students develop basic word-perception skills and word-attack skills, which give independent power in vocabulary building, but to demonstrate the possibility of reading for pleasure. When students discover that reading affords just as much of an escape from harsh reality as their rock 'n' roll phonograph records or television shows, then I feel their lives have been expanded and enriched.

I feel that we have had success with our reading program at North Carolina College because practically every faculty member contributes to and supports the program. This may be because the course has clearly disclosed the urgent need for improvement in the teaching of reading in our segregated Negro schools. This continuing reading failure marks a basic cause for many underachievers among our graduates.

For instance, I once had a boy with a marvelous I.Q. who made practically straight A's in all science courses. His whole life was wrapped up in science. He planned to enter the army and came to me seeking advice. I knew he had the I.Q. for Officers Candidate School, but felt a blind spot in his personal arsenal of general knowledge would trap him on his qualification tests. He had an absolutely woeful deficiency in the humanities. I proposed some cramming.

He came right back at me : "Why?"

"So you can score high enough to go to OCS," I said.

"Like what?"

"Let me give you a little test," I suggested. "Who frightened Little Miss Muffet away?"

"I don't know. Who's Little Miss Muffet?"

"One of the characters in Mother Goose."

"Who's Mother Goose?"

That part of this college boy which had been challenged, his interest in science, had grown. In the humanities, however, he had gained absolutely no knowledge, and the blame —if that is the proper term—extends all the way back through secondary and grade school to his childhood home. Furthermore, he had no present concept of having missed anything, nor did he have the slightest desire to learn what he had missed.

In so many ways the boy held much promise, and he was destined to go far. He went to dental school at Howard University and is now practicing dentistry in his home city in Michigan. I am sure he is still inadequate in the humanities, but is a member of the affluent society.

During those early days at North Carolina College I had to establish myself with my students. I also wanted to establish in their systems my standards for punctuality and responsibility. Traditionally at our campus, as at most Negro colleges, a student dropped in at a faculty member's office without a specific appointment and felt free to barge right in regardless of what you were doing. Or, failing to find the instructor in his office, but encountering him on the campus, the student would state his business then and there on the run.

I announced that all matters pertaining to the courses I taught would be discussed in my office and nowhere else, and that no student would be welcome at my office without an appointment. Furthermore, I would be in my office at the established time and would expect them to keep their appointment. When some appointments were forgotten, which happened often at first, I let this be known to the class, and made much of certain poor character-set habits of the Negro, habits which would have to change if they expected their abilities to prove of interest to employers.

At times my critical comments hurt a student's feelings, and I resorted to a lesson my mother had taught me. In my youth my aunt Lill was a boon to the Butler family and me in particular, but she had an uncanny ability to rub all of us children the wrong way. She thought nothing of opening and reading my mail, or going through my purse, or criticizing unnecessarily. One day she opened our closet and saw the many pairs of shoes worn or outgrown by five girls, and she fussed. "Poor people! That's what you are, and look at all those shoes. Sometimes I just can't understand Frances!"

Having no little girls of her own, Aunt Lill had no idea how rapidly little girls outgrew a pair of shoes. This we could forgive, but she had criticized our mother, and we did not permit that even from family members.

Henrietta said, "I don't see what affair it is of yours!"

Aunt Lill became deeply offended, and before any of us could get to Mother when she returned from work, Aunt Lill had told her version of the incident.

Mother called us girls together and very calmly said she thought we should all apologize to Aunt Lill. We said we didn't want to because we had meant what we said.

Mother replied, "I had hoped you could feel sorry for what you have done to your Aunt Lill, but if you do not feel you can apologize for what you did, you can at least tell her you are sorry that what you said hurt her feelings."

Thus, when a student unaccustomed to discipline and my insistence upon manners becomes ruffled by my direct approach, I recall this incident with Aunt Lill, and say, "I'm sorry if what I said hurt your feelings, but I meant what I said."

Not all pupils who enroll in our American colleges are prepared academically, mentally equipped, or of a disposition to profit from what college offers. For entirely too long the Negro community has failed to recognize that high school is not college preparation for all students. Many of these unprepared students would do better in a good up-to-date vocational school than in college. This decision should be reached in high school before the student who is not with the curriculum becomes a dropout. The fact that we have dropouts in no way means that such students have no aspirations or untapped abilities. But where can such Negro students go?

I have struggled with this problem and the long-overdue answer. Our high schools must offer those students who want it, while in no way degrading the student's own self-image (as we have done with vocational training in the past), the necessary training in a marketable skill. Today most of our high schools do not offer current technological areas of training. Our poor youths lack necessary funds and skilled guidance counselors to direct them to the training centers geared for their level of attainment. So where does the dropout go?

The advantages to the Negro colleges of modern and competent vocational training at high school levels would be tremendous. It would enable the Negro college to do a better job of leading their students in the transition from poverty-oriented education to the professional-cybernetics education needed in our country today.

For almost a decade now, since the emphasis on integration became the thing in educational circles, a straight-A or top-B graduate of an accredited Negro high school has little trouble securing a full scholarship from most good Northern schools, especially state universities. So the cream of our youth, those who have already been taught how to learn, are rewarded and taken off. Thus there flocks to the Negro colleges the remainder of the high school graduates who can meet even minimum entrance requirements. Many possess as much intelligence as their scholarship brethren; they just have never been taught the how and why of learning. But as their numbers increase, especially those who might be more profitably served by a technical curriculum, the faculty of Negro colleges find the pace of their classes held back.

The problem cannot correct itself. I recently read that in the seventeen Southern states for the year 1967, 45 percent of the eligible whites but only 15 percent of the eligible Negroes were going to college.

Maybe teachers should be less concerned with the question of where students go when they are flunked out of college, or when they don't go to college and have no marketable skill. However, it concerns me and I should think would concern America.

The Negro college has another trouble area, more in the social realm. When I attended the University of Rhode Island, my wardrobe consisted of three-piece wool suits, a sweater I had knit, several blouses, a pair of good sturdy cantilever shoes, and changes of underwear. We had a campus saying, "You have one outfit on your back, one in the drawer, and one on the line." Clothes were expected to be neat and clean, but were for warmth and protection. The

New England climate of course made wool suits quite suitable.

At most Southern schools, the students have tended to have a greater array of wearing apparel, and as a result of having a number of clothes changes, they have also tended to dress up. The art of dressing like a campus personality has proved to be an open sesame to social acceptance at most Negro colleges. With the right wardrobe serving as a passport to the "in" group on the campus, one may not feel the need to get down to study until it is too late.

Years ago I would have been critical of any girl who wasted an academic opportunity, and would not have been concerned with her environmental background. Today I recognize her as the product of a home where all around the children are growing up like rabbits in the raw, with little opportunity to see or experience intellectual benefits. Furthermore, what in our national life today would dissuade a girl from the belief that parading her female charms before the girl watchers is the aim of American womanhood?

Thus one learns that the Negro college works with the product of the Negro community, the variables of the individual parents, the levels of poverty and segregated education; all of which is somewhat altered by America's moral and ethical image of itself.

However, I believe we are moving into a more realistic era in North Carolina. Starting with the fall of 1968, a high school graduate seeking admission to a state college must score at least 650 on his SAT test. For the first time we should be picking out those pupils who can profit most from what college offers. I anticipate that the pace of our classroom work will decidedly pick up, and would hope that with guidance some present misconceptions about college life can be checkmated.

For those who fail to make 650 on the SAT, there are other Negro schools offering academic courses, and we need more such schools today.

In the South, the hordes of hopeful Negro students could not be absorbed by other schools right now. Nor could all of these students compete on larger, less personal, campuses. However, the fact that a few Negro colleges like North Carolina College can become more selective of student abilities should hasten some needed higher scholastic standards in the Negro community.

With higher scholastic standards maintained at some Negro colleges, I should expect them to become integrated, as did the schools I knew in West Virginia. Just this past summer we had more than fifty white students enrolled at North Carolina College. As we further improve our standards and capabilities, I expect more white students to take advantage of what we have to offer.

Church and Community

I moved to Durham to be with my husband and to teach at North Carolina College. But soon after I arrived there, I recognized the great challenge of furthering the educational opportunities of the three hundred young people of the Mount Vernon Baptist Church. Over the years, the church's children have provided the most rewarding aspects of my church-related experiences.

Mount Vernon presented a change from the Scott Street Church in Bluefield. There my husband had had an old-line church, whose congregation represented the established families and home owners, many of whom were two-car families. Although some of the college faculty belonged to that congregation, most heads of families were labor foremen on the railroad or in the coal mines. In the main, these workers earned more than the college professors, despite lack of higher education. Very few of the women of that congregation worked. By comparison, Mount Vernon's congregation consisted of two workers in nearly every family. They labored at the menial jobs in the tobacco factories, the hosiery mills, the flour mills, and in domestic service, and a majority did not own their own homes. The general level of education was no higher than that of Scott Street. But the compelling characteristic of Mount Vernon was this congregation's avid interest in any program which promised a better life for their children. Here was a church that would willingly make sacrifices today for its faith in a better tomorrow, if shown the way.

I reached Durham on June 5, 1948, and went to work at the college three days later, for I had signed a contract to teach six weeks of summer school. My work load at the college was heavy and left me no spare time, but the church would not wait. Once I had sensed the depth of the people's feeling, I did not want the church to wait. Therefore, commencing in July and continuing through August, I met weekly with the church's Planning Committee. We worked together harmoniously to set objectives and choose ways of training the children which gave greatest promise of success within our limitations of available funds and presently available trained volunteer workers. The charting of a new course has many pitfalls, but we cleared each hurdle which arose and proceeded with the confidence that we were making excellent plans.

The ten-hour-a-day work schedules in the factories presented the first major hurdle to our program plans. Most parents worked too late in the evening to go home and prepare supper for the children and then bring their sons and daughters to our study groups. Our plans called for such study groups to meet at the church for five consecutive nights from 6 to 8 P.M.

The committee solved this problem. They asked each of five Missionary Circles to prepare and serve supper to 350 children and adults for one night. Not one group hesitated when asked. The Planning Committee made the menus, the Circle ladies supplied and prepared the food. The children came to the church at 4:30 P.M. after school, lined up for meal service, and then prepared for classes.

Our second hurdle grew out of the failure of our State Baptist Association to cooperate. The literature for the courses had been ordered from the state association. The Monday the courses were to start we had no books. I drove to nearby Raleigh, and in the state association headquarters picked up whatever books they had in sight. I learned that that Baptist hierarchy did not look with favor on churches who planned and offered courses without the association's direct participation.

Out of this initial week's training came our Children's Church, soon to become central to all youth work in Mount Vernon Baptist Church.

The parents organized an Adult Council to be the policy-making body for the total youth-program work. We also set up an Educational Committee to promote a "stay-in-school-

and-go-to-college emphasis." I watched these people at work. I marveled at what they accomplished. This is why I know that with proper organization, participating and working through established channels, my people can promote effective educational goals even in such places described by the white press as the culturally deprived inner city.

One month after organizing the Children's Church, on November 8, 1948, the Mount Vernon Baptist Church Credit Union was chartered by the state. The church members present that evening invested $175, and the church's credit union was in business. Twenty years later that initial investment has grown to $62,487, and the credit union has become a constructive instrument in the improvement of the total life of our church membership. This has been especially true in our emphasis on higher education.

For example, I approached a parent whose daughter was about to be graduated from high school with the recommendation that the girl go to college. This father looked at me as though Sister Browne had taken leave of her senses, and asked, "Where would I ever get that much money?" We worked out an arrangement whereby he borrowed the money from the credit union. The daughter completed college with a degree in elementary education. She has been teaching in the public schools of Durham and now is a help to her family. She owns shares in the credit union, and even her son became a shareholder, when he was two months old. Another member sent three children to college with loans from the church's credit union, and many families have sent one or two children to college with this aid.

One church member came to the pastor with a proposition to make a sizable loan to enable him to purchase some lots in a section of the city that was just developing. The lots were

$400 apiece, and he wanted to buy three lots. The credit union loan made the purchase of these lots possible, and those lots are now selling for $1,200 each. On one of the lots the man has built an attractive and comfortable home that is an inspiration to all of our community.

The ability to borrow money for such purposes is called financing on the other side of town. Such transactions make the wheels of business go around, but only recently has credit at less than exorbitant rates become available to the black community. Therefore, the church's credit union, acting alone for most of these years, has enabled our people to improve their lot by helping them to help themselves.

Of course, the operation of the credit union has had its ups and down. Once we nearly lost $1,800 and had some anxious moments before the full amount of the loan was recovered. However, for the most part, the credit union has successfully provided money for education, hospital bills, real estate, home improvement, vacations, and the purchase of automobiles.

After the near-loss of $1,800, nobody wanted to be treasurer of the credit union. So, with the pastor's help, I was drafted. I am a good promoter and know how to take the money to the bank, but the auditor is convinced I have no talent or training for the job. What shakes him up is my method of operation. I don't ask for collateral if the loan is to a supporting church member. I simply know all of my accounts in terms of the people, their needs, and their situation. However, ten years of prodding by my auditor has taught me that every debit must have a credit—somewhere.

We are now trying to raise our assets to $75,000. For a group of unskilled workers, many of whom receive welfare checks, to acquire $60,000 in assets is in itself a source of pride. Although 65 percent of the members own only one $5 share, one member who worked in the tobacco factory has $2,000, and another who worked in the hosiery mill has $900. Ten people have more than $1,000 each. Dividends of 4 to 5 percent have been voted each year for the last eleven years. The credit union is a wonderful way to help one another.

Right from the start the pastor and I counted on the credit union to help the church's children go to college. As an added incentive to this educational emphasis, the Church Board voted to give $100 scholarships to any Sunday-school pupil who was graduated from high school and enrolled in an accredited college.

How to house our increasing number of children became our next church problem. When Mount Vernon Baptist Church was built in 1935, the point of view of the pastor and the church officers was of a pulpit-centered church. There were three small rooms in the church basement, which had been appropriated by adult Sunday-school classes. Our beginners met in a room beneath the stairs. The room had no windows, and the only light was provided by a naked light bulb hanging by a drop cord from the ceiling. A large hall was used for all other children's classes, and the deafening babble in this room, with all the teachers talking at once, only stopped when classes were dismissed.

The need for an education building was urgent, and a Building Committee, headed by Deacon Charlie Jackson, began a study of the programs to be housed in our educational plant. I had worked with the architect of the new educational building just completed at North Carolina College, and this experience proved most helpful in my work with the Church Committee. It took many meetings, some of them stormy, to overcome the underlying fears that we could not manage such an undertaking. However, this very real concern resulted in one of the finest and most complete buildings of its kind in Durham. Our building is fine because it was planned and designed to wrap up the ongoing youth programs of the Mount Vernon Baptist Church.

In our education building we have a children's chapel where children's worship services are held three Sundays a month. (On the second Sunday of each month, the children and their leaders worship in the front pews of the church sanctuary. The elder members move to the rear of the church and to the balcony and give first place to the children. Youth leaders from our Children's Church read the Scripture, pray, and present the speaker.)

As pastor of our Children's Church we have a student from the Divinity School of Duke University. The University's Field Service Department provides the minister, and Mount Vernon Baptist Church pays for a scholarship in the Divinity School. The scholarship varies from $70 to $100 a month. Only one year has the student minister been a Negro. As a result, our children experience a warm and friendly relationship with a young man of the white race with whom they can move easily. When one of our youth leaders looks at the young minister and says to the Mount Vernon congregation, "Our speaker this morning is *our own* Grady Wineger," that represents a high-water mark in our segregated society.

Many persons felt we should air-condition the education building to obtain maximum benefit of its pleasant classrooms, offices, kitchen, and lovely children's chapel. The pastor offered to borrow $5,000 on his life insurance policy and loan this money to the church. I was bitterly opposed to the proposition, although the pastor assured me the people would pay back the loan as soon as they could. I knew my husband, and know that he practices what he preaches and tolerates my more worldly and hardened point of view.

"Pastor Browne," I told him, "it is a good thing you have an employed wife. Otherwise, I might have to walk around outdoors in my bare feet in my old age."

Of course, the church repaid the loan promptly, and the pastor gave me that "I-told-you-so" look for at least a week. However, I was so relieved that I didn't mind one iota.

The next undertaking was a 100-acre recreation area twelve miles out in Durham County on the Boyce Mill Road. The Girl Scouts and Boy Scouts, not only from Mount Vernon Baptist Church, but the whole Durham area, camp there. The church holds cookouts and picnics there. The church organizations have improved the grounds and buildings and have even built a fish pond, which the state fisheries department stocks.

On our first all-church outing to the property, one member, a dear old soul, sat rocking and thanking God out loud. She said, "All this here belongs to us all. Can't nobody drive us out of here. The Lord has provided it for us." She rocked and talked and ate fish in complete freedom. That is what the possession of land, the feeling that a piece of God's green earth is yours, has done for men through the ages. It has made Mount Vernon Church secure. In case something happens in town, we have somewhere to go.

Mount Vernon Baptist Church's greatest asset is its people—wonderful, loyal, hard-working people. They participate in all the planning and implementation of plans. They know the value and necessity for dissent, and most of them can discuss issues and not personalities. Although I did not want to come to Mount Vernon Baptist Church, now nothing could make me leave.

North Carolina also presented a challenge in the community. In 1948, soon after my arrival, I visited the Girl Scout office and offered my service as an experienced Girl Scout leader. Scouting in Durham was a "we" and "they" proposition. Negro leaders were referred to as Negro Scouts, white leaders as Girl Scouts. There was nothing in the operational design to indicate that both groups were engaged in the same program. As a result of some smooth operating and an assist from Mrs. Mildred Amey, a fine Christian and splendid Brownie Scout leader, I became the first Negro on the Administrative Board of the Durham City and County Girl Scouts. My letter read, "You will attend all business meetings of the Board," which implied that I would not be expected to attend any social meetings. However, I attended all meetings, was well received, and made a contribution which I believe gained the respect of all the women.

Out of this experience I was appointed to the Committee for Planning the Area Council, which extended the coverage of the Durham Council to include a nineteen-county area with thirty-eight neighbor organizations, which in 1968 served 15,505 girl scouts and 2,081 adults. We leased a campsite and built a camp where Negro and white girls can enjoy Scouting activities at the same time.

At an International Girl Scout conference at Camp Edith Macy in Pleasantville, New York, I worked and planned with Scout leaders from all over the world. My awards include the coveted "Thanks Badge," the highest award the council makes for service. Later I was recommended and appointed to the National Field Committee for Girl Scouts.

To those persons who complain that Girl Scouting is a

good middle-class movement, I say: Get into Scouting and live by the Girl Scout laws. Then you will be enriched spiritually and your economic status will be transcended. Scouting for girls is fun with a purpose. Scouting for adults is lasting, enduring, friendship. If you meet a "body" in a Girl Scout uniform that does not reach out with a smile to another person in uniform, she is not "a friend to all" and consequently not a true Girl Scout.

When I assumed the responsibility of cochairman of the drive to build an addition to the Harriet Tubman Branch of the YWCA, I asked my Girl Scout friends to help. They came to my aid. Mrs. Barbara Schiebel, who was chairman of the Girl Scout camp program, gave of her time, talent, and money to our effort. Every Girl Scout friend that I asked made a donation.

So many people gave and worked for this cause that the whole city of Durham can take pride. Although this branch YWCA is designed for use in a Negro neighborhood, Durham worked as a team for the success of the drive. The United Fund gave a hearing and granted permission for a capital-funds drive and for special help in financing the building. Although there is complaint concerning lack of communication between the two races in Durham, and rightly so, sometimes and with some groups, interaction works perfectly. The Negro business community, the United Fund Administrative Board, and the YWCA Board, in this instance, demonstrated the value of talking together to get things done in a community.

Ever since coming to North Carolina I had been bothered by the fact this state had no public kindergartens. Long before Project Head Start, I knew that my children must have a good nursery-school background if they were to close up the educational gap and enter the race to catch up with the rest of America.

Those fifteen wonderful classrooms in our Mount Vernon Church educational building, sitting idle most days of the week, literally bugged me. For some time I had considered taking a lighter teaching load at the college. With a little manipulating I was able to arrange my college schedule so that every morning remained free for my nursery school at the Mount Vernon Baptist Church. I proceeded to hire a staff, to get state approval, and to operate at our approved maximum student level of fifty.

This nursery school does not operate as a conventional nursery school, where the patina of middle-class status is ever present. We must start with the poverty problems of the Negro community and the belief that early childhood education offers the most effective way to rescue the child of the slums from the cycle of failure which now awaits him.

To break the cycle of failure, we built our curriculum around love—love and more love. Furthermore, our curriculum is not determined by anticipation of later school needs, but by the nature and present needs of the individual child at the time we receive them.

The typical middle-class nursery school operates on the theory that programs can directly influence only the child's emotional and social development, not his mental growth. It is assumed the child's intellectual development will take care of itself, following a sort of built-in timetable.

Early childhood educators tell us that by the time a child reaches the age of six years, two thirds of his intelligence has been formed, with the most rapid growth taking place before age four. In the case of the poor, this means that what the child has not learned at home by age four must be learned elsewhere, and quickly.

The middle-class parent reads to his child, answers questions about labels, street signs, TV advertisements, coloring books, and takes the child to a variety of stores while shopping, and then answers a new variety of questions. In the middle-class home the parents use complex forms of speech. All of this constitutes a learning process which seems quite natural to the middle-class parent and to the public-school teacher, who also most likely has a middle-class background.

(Even the Negro girl who has risen out of poverty to the middle-class eminence of a teacher, seeks those values associated with her new position. She becomes critical of children from the slums where she had her origin. Of course, the Negro does not like to look back because for most the experience is not pleasant.)

What is so different about the home of the Negro poor? The children of poverty quickly learn that the best way to stay out of trouble is not to ask questions. In homes of the semiliterate, curiosity and questions are usually rewarded by rejection, since the adult doesn't know the answer and hates to be reminded of this insufficiency. In such homes, the parents indulge in a type of dialogue which consists of brief commands or phrases, often poorly enunciated. The conversation stimulates neither thought nor question. With transistor radios constantly turned up, poverty's child learns from an early age to tune things out, not to ask questions, and not to pay attention to words.

Thus, at nursery school we must start by finding a way to turn each child on, and to communicate by words. Love is the key to unlock the child who has been denied his childhood.

Once we have the individual child participating in our group activities, we introduce him to guessing games, sorting games, counting games; we look at multicolored pictures (preferably simply drawn) and talk about what we see. We read to our children and answer their questions. We blow bubbles and talk about why we have bubbles.

There are those educators who feel that to offer stimuli to move a child forward intellectually will somehow stunt the social and emotional development, to say nothing of robbing the child of his childhood. To this I say "nuts." Let those protesters visit my children, who have learned the alphabet and how to count to ten, and see how they are suddenly turned on with a thirst to learn more and more.

But really, these are not the areas which we stress. When a child becomes ready, then we like to see the joy of his self-discovery in some phase of intellectual attainment. This does something wonderful for the self-image of the socially deprived.

My nursery school takes children between two to six years, and operates from 7 A.M. to 5 P.M. We include a hot lunch, nap time, juice and crackers midmorning and midafternoon. We operate five days a week and the charge is $7.50 per week. However, no child can attend our nursery school whose parents (both parents if in the home) fail to come to our regular monthly Parent-Teacher Association meeting. The child finds it much harder to unlearn old habits than to learn new ones, so we constantly seek to upgrade the environment of the home. Failure to reach the home invariably slows down our progress with the child.

Each morning when permitted to do so, I join my assistant director, Mrs. Veave Faulk, and we greet the children as they arrive. We make a fuss over each arriving child and seek to show them that they are important. For the stand-offish type we offer our hand and say, "I'm glad to see you." Then we comment favorably on some part of their appearance which we can honestly brag about. The long-timers come running to us and say, "Give me a kiss." If a little shy, they are apt to say, "Give me a hug," but what they really want is to be kissed.

Until our P.T.A. has had some effect, many of those children experience no demonstrative affection in the home. They may not yet understand their blackness, but they sense that something is wrong. Into this doubt, which the parent himself does not understand, nor knows how to handle, we seek to instill self-respect and love to convey the idea that each child is important, is a person loved by God and by us.

Some of the new children are pathetic. We had one boy, four and a half years old, who wouldn't talk. We took him to the clinic and the speech therapist. There was nothing organically wrong. He simply came from a home where words were not spoken. One of my teachers did a marvelous job of patiently working with him through various stimuli until his desire to learn and participate outweighed his fear of speaking.

I am with the children every morning and those afternoons when I am not teaching at the college. When nap time comes I put a lullaby on the record player and tell the children they don't have to sleep, just rest on their cots. If I told them they had to sleep, they would fight sleep. However, I know and they know that Mrs. Browne will be the first to fall asleep.

One thing I think most adults fail to realize is how their

actions and attitudes affect their children. I recall an incident that happened when my son Emmett was in the first grade.

My husband and I had taken Emmett into our backyard to show him the night sky and the Big Dipper. While we watched the heavens, a large airplane flew overhead. We had been looking at the stars, but in typical childish change of direction, Emmett said,

"Hey, pilot drop a bomb on Russia."

"Why?" I asked.

"They're Communists. Communists are bad," he replied.

"Why are they bad?" I asked, the teacher in me coming to the fore.

"I don't know," Emmett replied.

We knew that as parents Pastor Browne and I had had something to do with our son's impromptu comment on world politics.

Adult words, attitudes, directions mark the course for our small children. How do we adults handle ourselves in the home? Are we positive or negative? Are we open-minded or are our minds set? Are we fair or selfish? All of these are directional signals, and we see their results in the nursery school.

Something else the nursery school often sees is the working mother who loves her child, but has so little time with him that no real parent-child relationship develops.

We had one little boy who responded so to our love and personal interest that he literally glowed with happiness. He soon became one of our best pupils. At a Parent Teacher Association meeting the boy's mother said to me, "Mrs. Browne, my boy just loves it here. All he talks about is Mrs. Browne's way of doing things."

This was too much of an opening to miss, and I thought I knew what the little boy had been trying to tell his mother.

"You work all day," I told her. "Your son doesn't get to see much of you. He knows you're his mother because you are worried when he is hurt. But you don't really play with him. Now my way is to grab him and hug him and say, 'You're my boy and I love you and we'll have fun together.' Go home and try it."

This mother did. She and her son soon enjoyed a new and natural relationship despite her hours out of the home. She came to me and said, "Mrs. Browne, your way works and is fun. Why didn't I think of it?"

Don't blame the working mothers for not trying. How about the upper- and middle-class home where the child is parked at the nursery school for the day and for reasons other than the necessity of work?

I recall another incident, a little girl who had become increasingly reticent and distant. The teachers report such incidents to me, and I spent several frustrating days trying to find the key to again reach this child. Then one day, when we were having cookies and juice, the little girl came to me and asked, "Mrs. Browne, may I have another cookie to save for my mother?"

With this opening I learned that the girl's mother was in Baltimore for several months, taking a course to upgrade herself for her job. The little girl had been left with relatives and was lonesome.

I found a large calendar and wrote the little girl's name on the face of the calendar. Then I showed her the day and the month when her mother would be home. We circled that day on the calendar. Then each morning we crossed off another day on the little girl's calendar. Her emptiness and lone-liness did not seem so endless then, for she could see on her calendar that the time was really growing shorter. In nursery school she again opened up and smiled and talked and played with the other children.

This mother, immersed in her own sizable problems and worries, had impressed on her little girl the month and day when she, the mother, would return. Never once did she realize that time had no specific dimensions or real meaning as yet for her daughter. After a few days of the mother's absence, that fear of parent separation that lurks like a cloud in the mind of our young became dominant in this little girl's thoughts. Fear increased daily until she was noticeably disturbed. Fortunately we found the key to her problem.

We have learned that the problems of our children nearly always have their origins in adult actions which have touched the child.

Among the many toys used at our nursery school there are no guns or military toys. Obviously we are fighting a los-ing battle here. The children go out on the playground and the first thing the little boys do is point a finger at someone and say, "Bang! Bang! You're dead! I shot you!"

I had had little boys come to me in tears. "Mrs. Browne, can't you make them let me be alive once in a while?"

It amuses me how the children never select the cowboy brawls, which are also prevalent on TV, as their method of exerting domination. Of course, you can get bruised and hurt in a rough-and-tumble cowboy fight. Much easier to point a finger and say, "I shot you! You're dead!"

Nor is it surprising that they play in this manner. Never in the lifetime of these children, and seldom if ever in the lifetime of their parents, has there been a period when there was not a hot war somewhere on this globe, with news clips of the real thing shown on TV broadcasts.

I am not a pacifist per se. My son Emmett serves in the United States Air Force and is now in Viet Nam. I don't cheer about it. I am a mother. But what worries me as I work with these children is this. How many more wars must we fight to end all wars? Is mankind too shortsighted, too lacking in resolve, or too greedy to stop fighting and give the world's common folk a few extra moments to find themselves in the affairs of today's society?

In the nursery school we spend a great deal of time reading to our children, trying to help these children—my children—find that they are human beings and can take pride in themselves. Frequently you will find me seated on the floor of a classroom, a group of children gathered around, their smiling brown faces looking up eagerly. The little girls vie for a place on my lap, and the little boys reach out and touch me and the bolder ones give me a quick hug.

We have the newest and latest award-winning books, and many older titles also. Frequently we let the children select the stories they want to hear read and explained. (I only wish I were as dramatic a monologist as the "storyman" back in my childhood.)

Unquestionably the most frequently requested books are the *Tales of Uncle Remus,* by Joel Chandler Harris, and the children's classic *Little Black Sambo.*

You should hear these poor little boys and girls laugh and carry on over these stories.

"That fox threw Brother Rabbit into the briar patch. Brother Fox ain't so smart," someone says.

"Brother Rabbit smarter than anyone else," announces another child.

"That briar patch was a trick," reports another.

The point I am making is this: These stories communicate, they have real story values which call forth active responses from these children of America's slums. The more these stories are read, the more they are requested.

Now some of our public school systems have removed these fine books from their list of approved curriculum materials. The persons who believe in this censorship can quote sociologists, psychologists, educators, and other highly trained specialists. All say these books are harmful to a minority race and will do this and that to the poor Negro child.

For the record, I personally selected these books for my nursery school. I still use them. To deny these children's classics to our Negro child because someone in the book is called black is to me a most tragic mistake.

It is just one more example of the syndrome of our times, which leads us to throw out the baby with the bath.

Just imagine a child growing up without knowing the real meaning of the phrase, ". . . throw him into the briar patch"? Or should we deny the Negro child the right to marvel at and to dream wondrous dreams of owning a pair of purple shoes with crimson soles and crimson linings?

Personally, I always thought Little Black Sambo was called black because that was the color of his skin. Certainly today's Negro children are going to be called black, for that is the color of their skin. (And I do know that the story setting is India, and I know what happened to the tiger.)

Now, if those persons who made the decision to discard these perfectly wonderful children's classics because the stories mention a black skin color, if these persons feel it is bad to have black skin, well then, that is something else again!

Of course, I tell people that I am as black as the Queen of Sheba and twice as pretty. I happen to believe, just as my High Priestess taught me, that the Negro race should take pride in its identity. Finding such identity in literature and educational stories, to feel that they are a part of the total life of their country, I believe helps build that identity in a positive way, while seeking to erase our Negro distinctiveness and individuality creates a negative self-image.

The educator's goal should be to provide a well-rounded education for the child, for every child, including the Negro child. This remains far more important—for the child, for the civil rights movement, for our country—than trying to find a *cause célèbre* in every little word or phrase.

Let me illustrate. I met Bessie Lyons in one of our public schools. She was a beautiful child with smooth black features and flashing black eyes. I discovered the teacher had just whipped a boy for calling Bessie Lyons black. I asked the teacher why. I wanted to know what was wrong with being black. The teacher didn't know. It was just in that teacher's mind that being black was bad, or a sufficient burden to bear without being reminded of it.

Now in my home, in a most prominent place in the living room, I have several African ivory carvings of native figures. The figures are portrayed with flat noses and thick lips. One of my Negro visitors looked shocked on seeing these beautifully and artistically rendered carvings.

"Why do you have those awful things, Dr. Browne?" she asked.

"Because they look just like you and me," I replied. "Remember, the sphinx has a flat nose and thick lips, and people have been raving about it for years."

Part of the problem is that the Negro race does not recognize its own history. When the ancient tombs along the River Nile were first opened, the jewelry discovered there was copied far and wide. The Negro, however, couldn't take pride in this original work because he did not recognize it as part of his history.

We may be making more progress in this direction of identity these days, now that some of our Negro entertainers are on TV.

For a long, long time in America the Negro has not been allowed to be an individual, only a mass image, but today this is changing. We have our standout performers, too.

We accomplish quite a little at my nursery school. We have even made some remarkable progress at our Parent Teacher Association meetings with some of the parents. Yet, the greatest single need is for my children not to run into middle-class white racism and find their emerging self-image denied and thereby destroyed. When destroyed it will be replaced, and we have seen in America what the frustration of failure does to my children over the long, hot summers.

Now back in the late 1950's, as the Federal Government pressed for more integration in our public schools, the textbook publishers had to undergo crash programs to prepare materials for this new situation. The textbook houses used many Negro educators to advise them how nearly one fifth of their fellow Americans lived and thought. I found myself working with a team of consultants for the Scott, Foresman Company of Chicago, Illinois.

Illustrations afforded the quickest and easiest way to integrate textbooks. Copy would come later. The illustrations were carefully planned to show neat, well-dressed middle-class white children and neat, well-dressed middle-class Negro children. The two races were shown together on the playground, at the zoo, riding on a bus; at the baseball game some of the players were shown as Negro athletes. There was nothing wrong with what was done, and it did mark a great step forward, but I kept wondering how some of my little children from the slums, who look as if they get their clothes from the Goodwill Industries grab bag, were going to find self-identity in those pictures. Also, suburban streets don't look like inner-city streets.

While working in Chicago, I also learned how deeply racism is ingrained in some people. The publisher was considering some original integration illustrations for teen-age textbooks. One series of illustrations disturbed each of the Negro consultants present. At first we could not put our finger on the problem. The Negro children, upper crust of course, looked like Negro children. The artist knew his trade. The illustrations were excellent in their rendition. None of the white persons present sensed our negative reactions to the drawings.

Then we discovered the problem. A Negro girl would be shown standing beside a white boy, white and Negro girls might be together in a group, white and Negro boys might be together in a group, but not once in some thirty drawings had the artist shown a white girl standing beside a Negro boy.

I felt sorry for the artist. I don't think he realized what feelings had lurked hidden in his subconscious. I don't believe he approached this assignment with any malice in mind. What we saw, and he had inadvertently revealed, was the result of a dominant culture in our country which has depreciated the Negro and held aloft white supremacy. It has made of the term "equal justice and protection of the law" a mockery, for, as every Negro knows, there has been integration of the races after dark since the first Negro women slaves arrived on these shores. Estimates of the numbers of mulattoes in this country run as high as four million. Now, if the act of integrating the races involved a white man and a Negro girl, the law has historically been rather impotent to render justice. The law appeared equally impotent if the sexes of the two races were reversed, for throughout the old South for nearly a hundred years that was cause for a lynching.

When I said we Negro consultants did not accomplish much, I do not mean to depreciate what the publishers did and have done since, or to deny that in this country there must be a basic concern for profits if a business is to stay alive. However, ten years later, with one or two noteworthy exceptions, the many textbook publishers still offer two editions of the same textbook to the school districts. One edition is integrated (some with Negro history included in the copy), and the other edition remains lily-white, as though one fifth of the population did not exist.

Thus, for my nursery child the best materials for self-identity remains the folk tales (and Uncle Remus is an American folk tale) and the animal stories. Although *Little Black Sambo* really relates to far-off India, my brown-skinned Negro children identify with the hero.

Upon my return from Chicago, I could not help teasing my husband.

"Pastor Browne," I said, "now that I am an educational consultant, I have a problem. As you know I've always tithed. It never was a problem to tithe on my salary as a Negro educator in the South. Now, Pastor Browne, since I've become a big consultant for a big publisher, well, they pay me a lot of money. A lot of money, Pastor Browne. My problem is this. The government takes a great big slice out of this new paycheck. Now I know what the Bible says about giving unto Caesar what is Caesar's and giving unto the Lord what is the Lord's. But, Pastor Browne, this Caesar is so much smarter than that earlier Caesar. . . . This Caesar takes his cut before I even see my pay. Now, Pastor Browne, my question is this: Do I pay my tithe on the stated amount of my salary—before Caesar takes his cut, or do I pay my tithe on the amount that is left over after Caesar has taken his cut? That, Pastor Browne, is my problem."

My dear husband replied, "Woman, don't make me regret that you came home."

However, it is North Carolina that has rewarded me. I could cover one wall in our home with plaques and citations. The reason they are all in hiding is that every one of them came to me as the result of the efforts of groups for which I had leadership. Although the plaques could never include the names of all who merited credit, instead of my name they should have been inscribed with the name of Charlotte Ann Elizabeth, my great-grandmother, who sent me out to achieve.

The most recent recognition came from the North Carolina Council of Health and Citizenship, headed by the eminent Dr. Andrew Best. The plaque says in the opening sentence: "Be it known to all people that Dr. Rose Butler Browne is held in highest esteem for her achievements as a leader, a teacher, a scholar, and an administrator."

The middle sentence would make my great-grandmother and my parents very happy. "Her many years of unselfish and unrelenting civic service on local, state, and

213

national levels reflect great credit upon her. She has few peers as a living inspiration for youth, and as a church woman."

I believe that this is the most significant honor that has come to me. Surely my resistance to moving to North Carolina was indeed a mistake. North Carolina was my assignment.

PART III

THE FUTURE

Chapter 8

EDUCATION

The recent Coleman report from the Educational Testing Service of Princeton, New Jersey, underscored several basic truths about our public schools.

1) The American educational system, as it now operates, is turning out seriously unequal citizens.
2) . . . the sources of inequality of educational opportunities appear to lie first in the home itself and the cultural influences immediately surrounding the home; then they lie in the school's ineffectiveness to free achievement from the impact of the home, and in the school's cultural homogeneity which perpetuates the social influence of the home and its environs.

To me the Coleman report shouts loud and clear that the learning process of every child is the resultant of the interaction of family, home, neighborhood, school, community, and nation. Of course, for the disadvantaged, this interaction involves a disproportionate dependency upon the motivating factors of welfare agencies.

In America we have federal, state, county, city, and private welfare agencies, and they are legion. I know of families listed with at least forty programs through a score of such agencies. Some welfare families appear to collect agencies and programs for the same reasons that more affluent citizens purchase blue-chip stocks—long-term security. The problem, however, is the lack of security analysts to determine which welfare programs are really beneficial.

The recipients themselves are not unaware of the confusion, overlapping, and often ineffectual total results. Recently I heard of an old granny who let a high-level group of poverty experts have it right between the eyes. "You're putting Band-Aids on a cancer!" she warned. Although her simile is not original, her diagnosis of the ailment and present prescriptions is most apt.

But the confusion does not end. Newspapers report of poverty specialists who want to expand welfare payouts until they reach a guaranteed minimum-income level, and then who will work when one can get it for nothing? There is talk in some circles of dropping mothers from the Aid to Dependent Children program when they continue to have illegitimate children, without regard to the financial cost and social consequence of the state's taking the childen and rearing them as wards of the state. Urban-renewal experts talk of rebuilding the inner city, and those who now live there start dreaming of new and rat-free homes, but the cleared land is sold for business developments and high-rise apartments which rent beyond the pocketbooks of the poor. Some educators advocate busing the poor to schools in more affluent neighborhoods, as though assuring the poor child (through his own eyesight) that he is indeed poor and disadvantaged will cure what ails him. And on and on extend the panaceas of do-good and get-well Band-Aids.

The effect of this present-day expertise compels me to remind myself, whenever I look back on my own childhood, that being poor does not necessarily mean you are disadvantaged. However, to be poor but not disadvantaged one must possess some of Charlotte Ann Elizabeth's inner drive and personal self-respect.

Now don't misunderstand me. America's poor, including a large portion of her Negro citizens, need help. This help will cost Americans more in taxes and personal involvement than most persons wish to recognize. However, to end poverty, to lift persons up to where they can see hope through their own efforts, is going to require some positive new thinking by all America. We must find ways to reach the inner person, and by unlimited patience entice individuals to want to achieve, and then through our schools afford such persons the opportunity to get the sort of education by which they can achieve. Failure to do so, quoting the Coleman report, means more "seriously unequal citizens," something America can ill afford.

What can be done?

The solution of the problems of the Negro in America must now come from the Negro himself. Not through proposals for new appropriations to relieve his condition, but from some fresh thinking about the problems which beset him and restrict both his self-image and his national image. Clear, cold, logical planning for action must then involve all Americans because the colored minorities are inseparable from the body politic of this nation. Nor is this an insignificant minority. By including the red, yellow, and black minorities, the total American colored population is greater than the total national population of North Viet Nam.

The focus of such national planning and action must be to coordinate all effort toward a share in the good life for all Americans. Such coordination points up individual, personal actions, necessary to positive participation in the progress of such programs in America today. The immediate areas for our concern must be:

1) *The good life demands a house that fits the family's size and style of living.*

Everyone in this country can support the new open-housing law. Not passively, but by extending a warm, firm hand of welcome to Negroes who move into one's neighborhood. Don't panic. You would be amazed, after your hasty sale before values go down, to learn what the Negro must pay for this same property through a broker. By style of living let me illustrate.

We criticize people just out of the rural South with its tenant farm shacks for their behavior in a modern high-rise apartment dwelling, which certainly is foreign to their knowledge and style of life. When the Wheat Street Baptist Church built its housing project in Atlanta, the Reverend William Holmes Borders insisted that each apartment have a front and back porch. He knew his people, so soon off the farm, would not feel at home without a place to rock and visit with neighbors.

2) *Support legislation to give Negroes the same civil rights other citizens enjoy.*

3) *Include members of other racial and ethnic groups in your social contacts. However learn to adapt to rejection on the basis of your race, for some colored persons are just as prejudiced as some white persons.*

These three suggestions are but a start of what can be done to support harmony between black and white America. However, their introduction in any community would represent the sort of positive attitude which could unlock doors for the vital problem solutions I wish to explore through the field of education.

The school is the agent of society, commissioned to do those things society wants done that are not the specific responsibility of some other agency or institution. It is reasonable, therefore, to include in our planning some special tasks for the school.

One writer suggests that the distortion of the Negro's past has always been done with a purpose. The insistence that the Negro has no history worth mentioning, this writer points out, is basic to the persistent theory that the Negro has no humanity worth sharing or defending.

Authorities are generally agreed that many Negroes, even small Negro children, show self-hatred, apathy, and despair. To say that black is beautiful is a pep talk to disavow this self-hatred.

Much must be done by our schools to correct this situation through the honest teaching of the Negroes' rightful place in American history. Such a curriculum change would reflect the contributions of the Negro race to American and world civilization. Failure to provide a fair representation of racial truths in present curriculum materials, most of which remain lily white despite television's success with the history of the Negro in America, has led some Negroes to advocate "all black" courses of study, an equal distortion of American history.

In attacking this problem, certainly those school texts which emphasize the moonlight-and-magnolia aspect of antebellum Southern history should be dropped from approved lists. A panel of representative scholars might build a textbook for junior and senior high school courses in American history in order to assure racial and ethnic fairness in all textbooks.

A fair recognition of the achievements and accomplishments of members of a child's race will make him proud of himself and of his race. He will take enjoyment in watching the surprise of members of the other races as they learn of the many firsts achieved by members of his people. A few of these achievements include the first open-heart operation and the development of the blood-bank system. Few people know that a Negro reached the North Pole with Commander Robert E. Peary, that thirteen of fourteen jockeys in the first Kentucky Derby were Negroes, a Negro invented the gas mask used in World War I, and a Negro invented the automatic traffic light for our city streets, to name but a few prideful firsts.

These and often even more commonly known facts are seldom taught in our public schools and may not even be known or believed by some of the faculty. I recall a discussion with the dean of a well-known graduate school, and this but a few years back, when he said to me, "Mrs. Browne, I had no idea that Duke Ellington was a Negro!" Television has largely altered the possibility of such an error in the field of entertainment today, but what about Negro accomplishments in other fields?

Today some states are in the planning stage to meet this need. Certain state legislatures have enacted laws calling for the development of representative content. Textbook committees have been appointed to select and order textbooks that are fair. In-service training programs are being conducted to prepare and assist principals, supervisors, and teachers in these new emphases in American History.

These are a few of the steps currently being taken. It would be well for all of us to remember that when this representative history emerges, it will not be like anything which you and I studied—it will judge a man for his achievements and not for the color of his skin.

Also, each school district should take positive action to make integration work in its facilities. To this end I would make four suggestions.

1. The members of the community, not just parents of the children in the school but people of goodwill in the community, should serve as a volunteer group to plan for success. Calls can be made on parents of children who are going into an integrated situation for the first time. Welcome these parents to the P.T.A. and school functions.

2. Ministers can help organize Sunday-school teachers and interested lay persons who can help such children and their parents to prepare the child's clothing, hair, fingernails, and personal grooming so that these boys and girls will appear as acceptable members of any group.

3. Student leaders should be encouraged to invite the new members to join clubs and try out for glee clubs and teams.

4. When tensions arise, astute people should arrange a

confrontation in which each group would be given a chance to tell what has happened. In this kind of learning situation, school people often find that the most disadvantaged white students, who are rejected by the more affluent whites, will take out their frustration on Negro students. As a result of face-to-face discussions, the faculty and staff will learn of the needs of each group, and tensions may be nipped in the bud.

Much valuable school time and faculty and staff energy is lost if children are thrown together without careful preparation, extended counseling, and guidance, until working and learning together comes naturally to at least 90 percent of the group. Remember, the Negro child who is already handicapped by so many environmental deficiencies needs the warmth and support of his peers and teachers if he is to profit by a more favorable learning environment.

Not long ago I visited an integrated grade school and at recess observed a lone little Negro girl in the third grade. Her back was against the wall, for she had become painfully aware that she had been excluded from all group activity. She was also being subjected to name calling. I could only assume that the little white girls were accurately reflecting the opinions and language of their parents. This started me wondering. If, in twenty years, this little Negro girl vented her now forming hostility and racial hatred by yelling "Get whitey," just who would be to blame, these children or their parents?

However, as a Negro and an American, I assume that in the other race there are persons of goodwill who are frightened and weary, as am I, of racial tensions and frustrations and are willing to seek fair and Christian means to alleviate this needless conflict in our American society. Let me, therefore, turn my attention on how best to prepare the Negro child and his family for their great step forward from their present agrarian and semiliterate state. We should first look briefly at a little history.

Early in the twentieth century the learned societies and the National Education Association were assigning to committees the task of building curriculum materials and setting standards for course work in the various disciplines. One eminent professor of education proposed that there were three factors conditioning the teaching process. They were, he thought: the child and his native equipment, the home and community life of the child, and the school with its limitations and advantages. Two generations later a prestige committee reported that the most important ingredient in a school was the young people themselves. Then more recently we had the Coleman report.

It should not be surprising to us, therefore, to find that our school systems as they now operate are turning out "seriously unequal citizens." The fact that the same group is always on the fag end of the distribution when achievement is measured, indicates that we must look beyond the school itself for some of the factors that are involved.

Findings which reveal these factors, as sources in the home and cultural environment of the learners, are not new to us. We have known about them, sighed about them, and with a shrug announced, "It's their background."

Once responsibility for the child's predicament had been safely shifted to the home, our schools, both segregated and integrated, felt this freed them from all blame in this tragic situation. In many instances, I have found conscientious teachers who, worried about individual children, visited their homes and purchased them lunches from their own

225

limited funds. Such teachers are trying to right a grievous wrong, but they are nibbling at the edges of the problem because they know no point of entry to the heart of the situation.

What disturbs such teachers is this. The only way to get good scores on the prevailing intelligence and achievement tests is to know the answers. The only way to know the answers is to acquire them in your environment. In your out-of-school or in-school environment the learning necessary to success on these tests must crop up. In fact, the two assumptions basic to intelligence testing are: (1) that each person who takes the test has had equal opportunity to experience the situations to which the test requires that he react; and (2) that each testee has had equal motivation to do his best.

In spite of full knowledge that neither of these assumptions is met, annually thousands of dollars are poured into testing programs to reaffirm the obvious—these children do not know the answers. Therefore, these children are adjudged lower in intelligence. If the ingredients that make up the apperceptive mass of the less-favored children were used as the stimuli in tests, the position of these children in the distribution would change. They would not be better off in the tasks of the school, but their performance on what they have encountered in their environment would point up the question and challenge us to answer it. That question is: Can we hope that children who are not middle class can succeed in a middle-class school, even when the society is purportedly classless?

The task of education involves recognition of the fact that schools in America are middle-class-oriented. In order to be successful in American schools, the skills, understandings, ideas, ideals, and values of middle-class America must be an integral part of the apperceptive mass. In America's poorer areas, children grow up in a framework of mores and folkways that provide various experiences, but not of the sort that helps them get on in integrated schools.

One way of meeting this urgent need is the provision of a program of early-childhood education that gears children for success in a world different from the one familiar to their parents. It also makes imperative the inclusion of the parent in the planning, for implementation of experiences regarded as essential to continuous growth and development of the child must be simultaneously experienced in home and school.

Havighurst and others have listed the tasks that children should achieve in the first six years of life. However, the fact that I ate with a spoon rather than with the utensils that society approves, when no utensil or only a spoon was provided by my environment, leaves a question as to whether I am backward or eminently successful. Anyone who can get black-eyed peas, grits, gravy, and side meat from plate to mouth with a bent spoon is not without skill of a kind.

With the framework provided by early-childhood-education specialists, reinforced by the learning necessary to fill known gaps in the development of disadvantaged children, a sound program may be started at three or even two years of age that will prepare such children for success in the American school.

Such a nationwide program is urgently needed.

What kind of teaching would be included to fill the gaps? Here is the morning circle for two-year-olds.

A chair in a circle for each child, with the child's first name printed on a large autumn leaf in September, a pumpkin in October, a turkey in November, a Christmas bell in December, will raise his appreciation of his own selfhood. He cannot recognize his name at first, let alone read it, but it is his. *My name, my chair, my teacher, my room, my bed, my place at the table. I must be somebody!*

In February, when the names appear on fat and round snowmen and are placed on a table, some of the children will be able to go to the table and select their own names. Others will not be able to do this, so we will help them—not by deflating their ego, but by saying, "You go to your chair, and I will bring your name."

An accepted Head Start activity today is to take the children on short trips, where they learn about new environments. All too often these are just trips, because no careful advance planning has been made.

At my school, a committee of parents and teachers visits our local Children's Museum, makes a list of things to accomplish on the nature trails, coordinates our reading to the program, decides what exhibits are most meaningful and can be further enlarged upon by class and home emphasis.

We visit the Children's Museum on the weekend and include a picnic so that the parents can attend. If the committee's work has been thorough and been followed through, there is much anticipation on the part of parents and children. It is indeed a learning experience, but the important thing to us is the fact that it is a shared experience between child and parents.

This shared experience provides the family something to discuss, something they did together, they learned together, they enjoyed together. Many of these parents have learned on this outing by the same method as a child learns, by asking questions. Hopefully, such a home will be more responsive to a child's questions in the future. Our great hope is to open dialogue between family members.

Another example of this is the spring party at our school. Here mothers and children play games together, and then have a fruit punch and cake. The games are blindman's buff, pin the tail on the donkey, and similar typical childhood party games. For the success of the party it is necessary first to teach such games to the mothers, who in many instances are unacquainted with such play activities. Nothing in their environment had ever exposed them to party-type games. Needless to say, the mothers enjoy our party as much as the children and love the games. This shared experience again provides for shared experiences and dialogue in the home. We know, for little children tell us how they and their mother taught their daddy how to play the games. We even have new mothers who ask us, as they register their children, when they will be taught how to play "those little games."

Many such experiences can be designed to increase conversation in the home and to improve the child's concept of himself, so that four years hence, when he moves into the first grade in the "big" school, with representatives of many ethnic and racial groups, he will walk in clean-limbed, cleareyed, and unafraid. He knows that he is prized and valued and knows that if he works hard, he can do what other people can do.

Emphasis on speech is also most important. Proper speech requires the understanding of parents. Parents who are not too knowledgeable about acceptable American speech will help by asking a child, "Is that the way your teacher talks?" Remember, the parents must be involved.

Recording a child's voice as he says, "My name is Charlie

Brown," in September and having him repeat a dictated sentence each month through January, and one of his own choosing each month thereafter through June, will make the child proud to hear his voice played back from the tape. He will become critical, first of himself and then of others. In this way, he will learn to develop standards of performance, to be constructively critical, and to hear the truth as others see it without flinching. Later, when some insecure white child says, "You are a nigger," he will answer, "No, I am a Negro American and proud of it!" He will have put this on tape so many times, at least four times during Negro History Week and at other times on special days and occasions, that he knows by now that people see things differently. All of this will come naturally in the speech work.

We think in words and the concepts they call forth. Reading calls for auditory and visual discrimination. In my school we work on these and other skills known to be basic to successful reading. We trace and sound letters and words made with emery powder on hot glue, to get the feel of writing. When we are ready, we read and write in the three-, four-, or five-year-old group.

We look at pictures of all kinds of children and books that show clean, pleasant Negro and white children in work and play situations. We studiously avoid books prepared by publishers who, in order not to offend the market, never place a little colored boy close to a little white girl, even in a picture, or publishers who show Negro children on the end of the lines in group pictures. We want the publisher to tell it as it is.

Children from a world in which it is necessary to watch and take care in order to survive, and who have been taught that everybody is after them, are more perceptive than many of us who are at ease. These children will notice and ask questions that cannot be answered.

It will take directed experiences to carry the disadvantaged child through the developmental tasks necessary to signal to all who encounter the child: This youngster is ready.

The effectiveness of the school in early childhood education, or at any level of education for that matter, is determined by the kind of home environment provided the child. Any child is better off if he is born to two people who love each other in a way that they don't want to love anyone else, and grows up warmed by that love.

The Negro child is more frequently dependent on his mother for love and sustenance; therefore any effort to affect the climate of the home will be more profitable if directed toward the mother.

The regularly constituted agencies that arrange the communications between school and home are suspect. Many poor parents believe that the P.T.A. is for affluent parents. They reject home visits by teachers, and assume that something is wrong when the teacher goes to the trouble of visiting.

There can be no wholesale approach that will attract all the parents or even those who need help most. Small groups made up of mothers who care for their children and have a spark of hope for the future of their families can be enticed to come and hear proposals about what we can do together.

It is a challenge to the leadership to get these mothers involved in meaningful experiences that will give them feelings of personal worth and a sense of accomplishment that will make them wish to continue. The first session might involve a series of checklists of developmental tasks—of preschool: birth to six years of age; the school years: six to twelve years of age; adolescence: twelve to eighteen years of age. After a discussion, choice of the tasks that the mothers wish to know more about for the sake of their children could be decided. Then the mothers might be encouraged to select some things that they might like to learn for their own sakes.

For instance, through such discussion groups in our school we have seen a too-fat mother learn that she would fare better with her teen-age daughter by losing twenty pounds. A mother who denied herself a hairdo in behalf of her girls learned that her daughters would take better care of their own hair when they had to share the available funds with their mother. Improving herself, her speech, her appearance could be the first step toward a mother's security and release from fears of inadequacy and rejection.

Other subjects requested include help in meal planning and wardrobe planning—making garments with easy patterns, remodeling clothing secured from clothing cupboards maintained by some schools, churches, or through purchases of used clothing from thrift shops. In most groups one woman would have a skill to share such as crocheting, knitting, low-cost meal planning. Sharing with others—eager giving and eager receiving—can be a shot in the arm for one who needs the spark of hope fanned to a flame.

No one group's endeavors can be a pattern for other groups. Only the goals will be the same: to arouse and nurture feelings of personal worth, and to understand and support the efforts of the school in behalf of the children.

Each group can serve as a leaven that will work through the community. Never will the groups be permitted to grow beyond a size that can meet easily in humble homes, and never will the program be one that could be regarded as in competition with the P.T.A.

The school cannot function as effectively with children whose personal lives are marked by barrenness, apathy, or hostility. Early contacts between preschool children and a program of education designed to meet their needs together with cooperation through the fellowship of work with parents is the only hope for American education in the foreseeable future.

Time is short, for today impatient black men engage in hot debates in many widely separated sections of our country. Some contend that America hasn't had any race riots yet, for the action so far has been mostly an emotional reaction by some poor Negroes against the hopeless contrasts between their lives and the lives of "everybody" else. Others contend that what we see is the start of a revolution.

Whatever name is assigned, whenever we have widespread national disorder, fear and mistrust are generated. Unless we acknowledge that there is a growing gulf between the races, a gulf that must be bridged if the American way of life is to survive, the schools cannot meet their real and total responsibilities. To put it bluntly, white America can no longer leave its moral responsibilities to be carried by proxy by a few agencies doling out dollars. The question is this: Is the Negro a part of America? And if not, what are the consequences?

Recently an irritated white woman in discussing her own feelings about rioting blacks accused the blacks of wanting everything handed to them, wanting to murder white people in their beds. As a matter of fact, when riots occur, it has been estimated by several high-level commissions that no more than 3 percent of the Negro population takes part in or even approves the tragic destruction. The tendency of some to lump all blacks together as an illusive "them" and to decide that "they" are the enemies, cuts off a sizable majority of responsible Negroes anxious and desirous of positive, workable, reasonable, and fair solutions to America's racial dilemma.

The investigations of these riots have revealed that many Southern migrants, Negroes on the move from "less to more," from "bad times" to "good times," felt that on their arrival in the North they had reached the Promised Land and everything would be changed. They had invested in a one-way bus ticket and a cardboard suitcase and held fictitious hopes of welfare support that was free for the taking. They had never heard of establishing residence. They viewed this law as a trick of the white establishment. Soon their dreams were shattered, and they felt defeat and total despair. They found they had exchanged the leisurely, informal patterns of living back home, which included occasional jobs to help keep body and soul together, for a fast-moving, time-clock-punching, dizzy pace of living that demanded working all day long every day if anybody would give you a job. The harder they struggled to eke out a living, the more frustrating it became. Despair can turn to hatred and a spark of conflict to a flame of destruction.

The unjust local laws, the savage private discrimination from which they had fled, were nothing to the automation and industrial development of the North which reduced the need for unskilled labor to the point that many of these black men were not only unemployed but also were unemployable.

This dreary picture is becoming all too familiar to America. Many earnest people, blacks and whites, are deeply concerned, but find the apathy of ignorance and selfish self-interests blocking constructive steps.

There are those persons who wish for the good old days when "colored folks" were trusted servants, who lived in the house like one of the family. That day will never come again. Negroes are not going to be satisfied with the white man's leavings any more.

Others want us to understand what slavery and privation has done to the poor Negro, "who had no heritage to spur them on like the white immigrants to America." Such people have forgotten their history. Prior to the Revolutionary War, many of America's white immigrants were England's criminals dumped across the Atlantic, or else individuals who had sold themselves as indentured laborers, for a given number of years, to pay for their ocean passage. They have also forgotten that Caesar sold blue-eyed Saxons in the market place in Rome; that the Huns, Vandals, and Goths came down on the great Roman Empire and in five hundred years had amalgamated with the people. If we must look for causes, the principal one lies much closer to our period of history.

The effects of slavery in America are remembered by people now living. The quality of the kidnapped African, able to withstand the rigors of trans-Atlantic passage on slave ships and sunup to sundown field work, was one of remarkable physical and mental courage, and their descendants are today's Negro Americans. All too often these descendants, aware that their parents were stripped of selfhood, economic opportunity, and equal educational opportunities (in this land of the free and home of the brave), see a continuation of the problems of the past. They note the slow pace of change in racist discrimination, and individual hope fades as they reach adulthood in homes devoid of the stimulation of intellectual growth. Imagine a home without books or exchange of thought! This is the problem now faced by our schools, and this problem must soon be answered by America.

The school organization is an administration device to promote the education of children and to facilitate pupil and school accounting. In my opinion, two important administrative changes must be made by the school to help these disadvantaged children close the existing educational gap which separates the races.

The first new step is to recognize the schools' share of the responsibility to change the child's environment in the home, along with other agencies, so that the disadvantaged child starts the "big" school with a background which enables him to learn in a middle-class school environment.

The second step, I feel, is to adapt the 4-4-4 school organization, which seems more favorable for teaching and learning situations and the promotion of pupil retention. However, all is for naught unless the preschool training—with child and parent—which I have discussed is instituted to prepare the child for this experience in learning.

In the first four-year grouping, I would favor lengthening the school day from 8:oo A.M. to 4:30 P.M. for the second, third, and fourth levels. Since more things are to be done (certainly in the disadvantaged areas), more time will be required. Too, the unstructured time for neighborhood activities will be confined to weekends, and the school week will be just that.

In these first four grade levels, I believe in seeing that the child progresses as fast as his abilities permit—he may reach the prescribed level of attainment in three years, four years, or five years. The important fact to be remembered is that he has achieved success in the disciplines set forth by the curriculum.

To do this I favor improving the existing neighborhood school from something less than first rate to first-rate level. I don't think de facto segregation is as important as first-class education. Therefore, I do not favor busing students to more affluent areas—as previously mentioned—because the basic causes of their disadvantaged status have not been remedied. Also, by lengthening the school day there hardly remains time to transport such young pupils as found in this first grouping of four grades.

Thus I envision the pupils' working hours spent in the school environment. A hot lunch will meet one third of his dietary needs for the day, and should be supplemented by midmorning and midafternoon milk and snacks. Medical and dental-health services will be a part of the program. Working through the neighborhood school with preschool graduates, whose parents are accustomed to shared learning experiences, heightens the school's potential for teaching reading and further involving the family in a growth situation.

In the middle four years, among new courses needed in the line of our discussion, is an economics course on "How We Spend Our Money." In other words, managing money with the needs of the Negro family in mind.

The members of the Home Economics Department of North Carolina College gave a short course in money management to welfare recipients in a Baptist church in Durham. Each person was given play money equivalent to her welfare check. A checklist showing things for which the families spend money was set up for each family. The envelope system was used to set aside money to meet the needs checked. Newspaper advertisements were used to weigh values in buying food.

Many of these families had spent their welfare checks within a day or two of their receipt, and these families then went the rest of the month borrowing from others or buying with a "store book" (on credit at neighborhood stores). Thus these families often had to be shown how to save a month's expenses from welfare payments before they could shop for bargains at discount and chain stores. Also, there was the problem of teaching these women how to store food if they purchased quantities at a discount.

However, if children and parents gain this information, the shared experiences will improve family fellowship, as well as stretch the family budget. The newer knowledge of money management will increase security and serenity in family living.

There are many such practical courses, which need teaching in these middle four years, as well as certain normal disciplines found in present curriculums.

In the four years on the third level, the group will be divided into college preparatory, and those who plan to develop a marketable skill during this four-year period. The offerings for the latter group will demand arrangements with local industry for school credit for on-the-job work.

In my own work at this level, I have learned that it is not enough to have teen-age girls visit an integrated office and see Negro girls at work. It must be pointed out to them, and discussed afterward, how these office-workers dressed, wore their hair, and fixed their fingernails, besides discussing the office requirements for the number of words per minute for typing and shorthand, spelling proficiency, etc. We brought along the girls' mothers on one such visit and were amazed at how this shared experience opened new avenues of discussion between parent and child. Mother and daughter had a reasonable and shared objective to concentrate upon, and were themselves witnesses to this real opportunity to get ahead.

Programs such as Diversified Occupations and Distributive Education, which are government-subsidized, can meet the needs of this second group when administered with some ingenuity and creativity.

The schools in the upper South and the border states are rapidly integrating. Pressures from the Department of Health, Education, and Welfare are spearheading wholesale movements of entire junior high schools, involving hundreds of children from Negro and white schools. The Negro students who gear into the new system at the seventh-grade level will have six years in which to catch up on many areas peculiar to middle-class environment and education. These children may require extra emphasis on speech, both articulation and enunciation; oral and written English, and vocabulary study; and physical and health education—physical fitness.

A good teacher meets her learners where they are and attempts to carry them forward. When children present needs too special to be met in the usual class organization and the legal school day, adaptations must be made to the needs of the learner. Such adaptations must be made in ways that will preserve the child's self-respect and protect the integrity of the teacher. This is no inconsequential task.

In essence, this "doing" calls for going over, under, or through barriers that seem insurmountable. The Negro is ingenious in handling concerns that matter to him; the American people have a resiliency that has withstood wars, pestilence, disease, failure, and frustration. In the last few years we have all learned that standing poor people in a line and throwing millions of dollars at them will not make them bend to pick them up. What will make them strive? Understanding what it means to be an American. To know conclusively that there is hope even for the poor.

If you learn only the difference between being poor and being a "poor thing," your perspective has changed. This difference, between being limited in your possession of material things and being poor in spirit, may enable one to go to Harvard, be graduated and elected to the honor society. It could even make one useful to this great country. This prospect seems so preferable to our continual negative attitude about the poor that I wonder why this great nation doesn't get started now.

Of course, to start now means to change one's attitude, the most difficult of all alterations. This is particularly true of the earn-more and spend-more middle class, whose economic security appears threatened by major shifts in national and sociological attitudes. To tell such persons that being their brother's keeper is going to cost them more of that dearly won green stuff is indeed to upset and challenge the present and prevalent attitude of America.

However, America must experience—through her churches, all media of communication, and all levels of learning—a metamorphosis in our responsibility-centered thinking, or the implacable lines of nihilistic and fateful confrontation now being drawn will progress beyond the point of recovery by measured and considerate decisions. These lines of open conflict, which have already started with the polarization of racial divisions, will rapidly change from racial separation to the more basic factor—the separation of the haves and the have-nots. If I want two automobiles and two color television sets, it is not the color of my skin but my ability to pay that decides the issue. If I am unable to pay, and realize this personal failure reflects in major part a failure of my out-of-school environment (home and community) as well as the failure of my in-school environment to prepare me for success, I readily turn to other means than those approved of by recognized society to attain my goals.

America, wake up! The reason your poor cost you more and more is that you give them less and less of yourself. By ignoring these your brothers and delegating their care to the elected politicians, and the legions of bureaus and agencies, you have displayed a penchant, yes, an avid and primary desire, to respond to the pitiful nagging of your conscience with impersonal dollars, rather than personal help and human warmth.

Welfare has become a profession. The poor represent the mass residue of a hateful system. It is not democracy that is hated—the poor have never known real democracy—what is hated is the inhumanity of man to his fellow man in terms of personal involvement.

America, the poor do not need your dollars nearly as much as they need your presence, your affirmation of concern and willingness to help, which alone can signify hope of a better day—in this democracy, in this nation, even for America's poor.

Nor will the vigorous presence of the poor let us forget them. If they do not love the present form of democracy in the same way as you and I, whose fault is that? Who were the teachers of the poor, yesterday and today? Who gave them lily-white textbooks? Segregated unions? Restricted housing codes? Jim Crow laws? Impoverished and sepaate school systems, or even just impoverished school systems? Police who seek to protect us but not them?

America, your poor will never think like you, until they know you really care. The Golden Rule may indeed be idealistic, as man has tried to prove for some two thousand years. But this same failure to put forth a hand so that the poor might pull themselves up, this failure to be concerned for those who lag behind in the parade of individual success may sow the Armageddon of our national fate with the same finality as the hydrogen bomb.

Successful America, wake up! Keep your dollars. Your poor brothers want to grasp your outstretched hands, and, encouraged by the love of your heart, start their journey to success.

INDEX

243

Index

Index

Rockefeller Foundation, 8, 19, 20

Rogers High School, 95, 96, 98, 99

Rolfe, John, 34

Rothney, Dr. John, 149–150

Ruth (pupil), 146–147

Rutland Street School, 70, 72, 73

Sadgwar, Elizabeth, 146

Schiebel, Barbara, 199

Scott, Foresman Co., 210

Scott Street Baptist Church, 158

Seay, Jimmy, 164

Shepard, Dr. James E., 168, 170, 171, 177

Smith, Jimmy, 143

Smith, Captain John, 34

Teachers' College, Columbia University, 18

"The Place," 63

Thompson, Mr., 97

Tidball, Benny, 21–22

Tidball, Henrietta, 21–22, *see also* Butler, Henrietta

Tuskegee Institute, 122

University of Rhode Island, 109, 110

Vial, Mrs., 70, 71

Virginia Normal and Industrial Institute, 111

Virginia State College, 5, 7, 8, 13, 116, 117, 118, 119, 126, 128, 129, 130, 137, 141, 144, 156, 166

Wade, S. L., 164–165

Wadsworth, Dr. Marcus, 94, 95

Walls, Alice and Hannibal, 173

Washington, Booker T., 122

West Virginia State College, 160, 161, 162, 163, 165

Weston, Kelly, 36, 37, 40, 42, 47, 52

Whiting, Dean, 166

Whittier, John Greenleaf, 87

Winning Farm, 56, 86

Winston Street School, 23

Worthington, Marguerite Lingham, 141–142